SPIRITUAL
PERSPECTIVES ON
GLOBALIZATION

SPIRITUAL

PERSPECTIVES ON

GLOBALIZATION

Making Sense of Economic and Cultural Upheaval

Ira Rifkin

Foreword by Dr. David Little,
Harvard Divinity School

Walking Together, Finding the Way
SKYLIGHT PATHS Publishing
Woodstock, Vermont

Library of Congress Cataloging-in-Publication Data
Rifkin, Ira.
Spiritual perspectives on globalization : making sense of economic and cultural upheaval / Ira Rifkin.
    p.   cm. — (Spiritual persectives)
Includes bibliographical references (p.   ) and index.
ISBN 1-893361-57-8 (pbk.)
1. Globalization—Religious aspects. I. Title. II. Series.
BL65 .G55 R54 2002
291.1'78—dc21

                                                              2002013687

10 9 8 7 6 5 4 3 2 1

Manufactured in the United States of America

SkyLight Paths Publishing is creating a place where people of different spiritual traditions come together for challenge and inspiration, a place where we can help each other understand the mystery that lies at the heart of our existence.

SkyLight Paths sees both believers and seekers as a community that increasingly transcends traditional boundaries of religion and denomination—people wanting to learn from each other, *walking together, finding the way.*

SkyLight Paths, "Walking Together, Finding the Way" and colophon are trademarks of LongHill Partners, Inc., registered in the U.S. Patent and Trademark Office.

Walking Together, Finding the Way
Published by SkyLight Paths Publishing
A Division of LongHill Partners, Inc.
Sunset Farm Offices, Route 4, P.O. Box 237
Woodstock, VT 05091
Tel: (802) 457-4000   Fax: (802) 457-4004
www.skylightpaths.com

To Jesse, Brady, Jody, Chelsea, and,
especially Ruth, my wife and rock.

CONTENTS

FOREWORD

THERE IS A WIDESPREAD BELIEF that the negative effects of globalization, particularly on economic and financial life around the world, are as severe as they are because of the absence of an effective counterweight. At one time, the labor movement was a barrier against many of the crueler aspects of corporate capitalism, as were the various versions of socialism that once existed. But those movements had their own problems, and in all the industrial democracies today, the labor movement is a pale shade of its former self, while socialism (along with communism) is taken to be mostly discredited.

With the resurgence of religion, some people suggest that the world's faiths are a promising substitute. This is a proposition that needs to be tested, and one of the great virtues of *Spiritual Perspectives on Globalization* is that the book effectively initiates that process of testing. In the pages that follow, Ira Rifkin provides, in an accessible and appealing form, some of the raw material by which to begin to determine how potent, how effective a counterweight to globalization the world's religions (or at least eight of them: Catholic and Protestant Christianity, Islam, Hinduism, Judaism, Buddhism, Bahá'í, and Tribal and Earth-Based Religions) might be.

In a way, *Spiritual Perspectives on Globalization* represents a two-fold challenge. It pulls together a recurring set of criticisms and objections to the inequities and injustices in wealth, working conditions, and quality of life, as well as to environmental degradation and the exercise of "unaccountable power" (in the elegant phrase of one of Rifkin's interviewees) that are, as Rifkin makes clear, associated with globalization in the minds of many religious believers across the world. The book forcefully conveys the impression that there is widespread and intense concern in all of the religions represented about the ill effects of globalization, and about the need to counteract those ill effects in various ways. These shared themes might well become a "platform" for effective common action, though, as the material in the book also makes clear, things are only at a very preliminary stage.

On the other hand, the information conveyed in *Spiritual Perspectives on Globalization* presents a challenge to the religions examined, as well. While there is evidence of broad inter-religious consensus on the objections to globalization, at least among some members of each tradition, there is also evidence of significant division within the traditions, especially the Roman Catholics, the Protestants, and the Jews, as to how negative the impact of globalization actually is, and whether it might not have considerable benefits as well. If there is to be a "united front"—requisite, one would think, for providing an effective counterweight to globalization—these differences and divergences will need to be confronted and to some degree harmonized within as well as among the world's faiths.

Moreover, if religious responses to globalization are to make a difference, cooperation of a practical, organizational sort will need to be expanded along with more theoretical interaction. The labor and socialist causes were, above all, organized political and social movements. Religious people will have to begin to reflect on and learn from the efforts of movements like those to curtail the excesses of capitalism (both the successes and failures), if they are to come to play the kind of influential role many adherents described in this book desire. An important start toward that end is valuably reported in Ira Rifkin's engaging book.

Dr. David Little,
Professor of the Practice in Religion,
Ethnicity, and International Conflict;
Director of Initiatives in Religion and Public Life,
Harvard Divinity School

PREFACE

THIS BOOK IS NOT MEANT TO EXHAUST all that may be said
about so multifaceted a subject as spiritual and religious
perspectives on globalization. Instead, look upon this book
as an introduction to how concerned, informed people in
many of the world's major spiritual traditions address the
complexities that surround the issue that may be said to
define the age in which we live. No attempt has been made
to include every perspective within each of the eight traditions profiled.

At the back of this book is a list for further reading on
the subject from a wide variety of viewpoints. Dip into it,
learn more about globalization, and seek out opinions I've
not included. Education is paramount for informed judg-
ment, and how we react to the sweeping changes that are
altering our world irrevocably will determine our, and our
children's, futures.

The book begins with a look at Roman Catholic perspectives because of the wide impact that the Church of
Rome has on the world stage. It ends with Protestantism
because contained within that tradition's myriad perspectives is a mirror of the virtually endless range of opinions on
globalization that exist within faith communities. The
remaining chapters are arranged, more or less, in alignment
with the tradition's contemporary potential or historical

contribution with respect to globalization. However, because each chapter is self-contained, the reader should feel free to read them in any order he or she desires.

Two final points. This volume is a product of primary research gathered through interviews and by attending forums, demonstrations, and other gatherings, both pro and con, at which globalization was the focus. Much was also drawn from the writing of various commentators listed in the endnotes and list of further readings. Finally, some readers will notice that diacritical markings are missing on words that normally require them (for example, the Sanskrit terms in the chapter on Hinduism). While many diacriticals were retained, others were intentionally dropped to make it easier for the majority of readers who might be unfamiliar with non-European languages.

Introduction:
WHY THE PASSION

ON A BRISK SATURDAY MORNING, Bonnie Phelps and Janet Dorman awoke before dawn to catch a public bus that would take them from great poverty to incalculable wealth in about forty-five minutes. From 125th Street in Harlem, America's most famous black ghetto, the bus traveled south through Manhattan's Upper West Side before swinging east toward Park Avenue, among the nation's most famous of moneyed streets. Along the way, the bus groaned its way past a polyglot of ethnic restaurants, dozens of houses of worship representing both the old and new dimensions of religious America, and sidewalks crowded with faces displaying a full palate of racial tones—all attesting to New York's place as a truly global city.

Phelps and Dorman—the former a retired African American public librarian, the latter a retired white public school teacher—made the trip downtown with a handful of others from their church, St. Mary's Episcopal, a historic Harlem congregation with a long record of liberal activism. On this day, February 2, 2002, Phelps and Dorman would push that history a tad forward by joining some seven thousand demonstrators on the streets around the posh Waldorf-Astoria Hotel. Inside, more than two thousand representatives of the global power elite had paid more than twenty-five thousand dollars each to attend the World Economic Forum (WEF), the invitation-only, annual gathering dismissed by the demonstrators as little more than an international cabal intent upon greedily dividing up the wealth of nations, and caring little about the consequences for the powerless.

Most of the demonstrators were half the age of Phelps and Dorman. There were hard-edged young men in crash helmets, self-styled anarchists seething with anger and itching to clash with the thousands of police on hand. In the aftermath of the terrorist destruction of the World Trade Center just months earlier, New York law enforcement was in no mood for radical dissent from the established order, and anyone who strayed from the fenced-off sites for allowed protest was swiftly cuffed.

The women of the Pagan Cluster were also there, chanting, "One heart beating, one people, one earth," as they rhythmically banged on pots and turned marching into choreographed dance. Police listened warily as the cacophony of shouted objections grew. "U.S. out of Afghanistan!" "Money for jobs not war!" "Stop corporate greed!" "Bin Laden, Saddam, Pinochet: All created by the CIA!" "End racism!" "Earth and animal liberation!" "No to genetic engineering!" "What about the workers?" "Cancel Africa's debt!"

Most of all, though, the invectives were directed against "globalization"—the current catchphrase for the complex economic and cultural changes that are transforming the world, reaching down even to its most remote corners. "9/11: Payback for Globalization?" read one sign I saw, just after a fifty-foot "WEF dragon" held aloft by demonstrators pranced down the street like a stray from a Chinese New Year celebration.

Daniel Yergin, the Pulitzer Prize–winning authority on international affairs, took note of the rising anger toward globalization at one WEF session. Coming from someone so steeped in the issue, his reaction might be seen as dismissive, or wildly oblivious to the depth of discomfort that globalization has generated: "For me, the amazing thing in a way is that there is so much passion about a word that has five syllables, [and is] about an abstract concept."[1]

What is globalization, and why do so many people—including many people of faith who see ultimate good, and even God's hand, in the process—share concerns about how it is unfolding, and, like the demonstrators, blame it for so much?

Abstract as it may be, globalization can be said to encompass certain elements. In the economic sphere,

> What is globalization, and why do so many people—including many people of faith who see ultimate good, and even God's hand, in the process—share concerns about how it is unfolding, and, like the demonstrators, blame it for so much?

globalization refers to the recent decades' unprecedented flow of capital and commerce across national borders, leading to the hegemony gained by international financial markets and multinational corporations, abetted by transnational agencies and organizations such as the WEF, the World Bank, the World Trade Organization (WTO), and the International Monetary Fund (IMF).

On a cultural level, globalization refers to the spread of what has been pejoratively termed "McWorld"—shorthand for the Western-oriented (many say American) global mono-culture that is burying countless regional and even national cultural expressions in an avalanche of MTV, Disney, Michael Jordan endorsements, and, of course, McDonald's-style fast food.[2]

On an individual level, globalization is about the pro-motion of consumer values that feed on the perception that happiness is rooted in material progress, that choice equals the highest freedom, and that being well connected is more important than being deeply connected. All of this has been pushed at a dizzying pace by the extraordinary recent advances in information and travel technology that seem to mock time and space. The end result is the trans-formation of human society to a degree and in ways not yet fully understood—but deeply disturbing nonetheless to many who worry about the growing divide between rich and poor nations, the commodification of life's basic resources, and consumerism's steady ascendancy.

In truth, though, the only things new about globaliza-tion are the phrase and the speed at which it is now occur-ring. Humans, in the parlance of the day, seem hardwired to seek the next valley and make it their own. We've been spreading around the globe and taking over since our ancient ancestors ventured out of Africa, perhaps as long as a hundred thousand years ago. Hunters and gatherers did it in their day. The early agriculturalists slashed and burned their way across the landscape, in some cases leaving it irrevocably changed. Greeks, Romans, Arabs, Chinese, Columbus, the conquistadors, and the Hudson Bay Company all pushed the globalization envelope, even if they did not always understand the globe's full breadth.

But globalization as we know it may be traced to a 1944 meeting in Bretton Woods, New Hampshire, at which representatives from forty-five nations sketched out a plan for post–World War II economic recovery. In doing so, they created the IMF and the International Bank for Reconstruction and Development, better known as the World Bank—institutions that critics charge are responsible in good measure for the economic, environmental, and cultural fiascos they cite as proof of globalization's systematic wrongs. International trade rules were liberalized and the flow of capital turned national borders into sieves. Soon, new media and new modes of transportation revolutionized the way we defined foreign and distant. A global village was upon us that more and more resembled an American buffet table—even if chilies, chutney, and kimchee were added to the mix.

Globalization's cheerleaders took to speaking of it in quasi-messianic terms. "The fact that free trade is now becoming truly global is one of the most important achievements in the history of mankind," says Edwin A. Locke, a

prominent behavioral psychologist in the mold of rationalist philosopher and novelist Ayn Rand. "If, in the end, it
wins out over statism, global capitalism will bring about
the greatest degree of prosperity and the greatest period of
peaceful cooperation in world history."[3]

Not everyone otherwise bullish on globalization is so
sanguine, however. Among the luminaries of the global elite
expressing second thoughts are Nobel Prize–winner and
former World Bank chief economist Joseph E. Stiglitz and
legendary international money manager George Soros.

Here's Stiglitz: "The West has driven the globalization
agenda, ensuring that it garners a disproportionate share of
the benefits, at the expense of the developing world.... The
result was that some of the poorest countries in the world
were actually made worse off."[4]

And Soros: "Many people, particularly in less-developed
countries, have been hurt by globalization without being
supported by a social safety net; many others have been
marginalized by global markets.... The heedless pursuit of
profit can hurt the environment and conflict with other
social values."[5]

Perhaps the backlash against globalization was
inevitable. Monumental change came at such an extraordinary pace that humans and their institutions were unable to
keep abreast. And whenever the human reality gets far
ahead of human psychology, a sizeable negative response is
assured. Not surprisingly, free-market capitalism, globalization's underlying ethic, became the target of that backlash.

As with globalization itself, anticapitalist sentiments
are also decidedly old hat. But globalization, say its more

anti-capitalist opponents, has pushed the free-market system into such high gear as to make it more Darwinian than ever. "It's like we now have capitalism on speed; it's rapacious," says Bilal El-Amine, a New York activist who edits an "anti-neoliberal" journal—neoliberalism being his preferred term for globalization. "It gets into everything, and turns everything into a commodity. It's done such harm it's given us a new New Left."

El-Amine is on the radical end of the new "internationalé," the globetrotting anti-globalization demonstrators (O sweet irony!) who turn up in the streets of Seattle, Quebec, Genoa, Davos, Washington, Calgary, New York, and wherever else the organs of globalization attempt to meet these days. Bonnie Phelps and Janet Dorman, on the other hand, are decidedly middle class and middle aged, and, they are quick to emphasize, by no means regulars at demonstrations. Yet there they were that Saturday in February, hanging in the cold with the radical fringe, at least for a couple of hours anyway. That's how long it took for the wind-chill factor to get the best of them and send them looking for a coffee shop in pursuit of hot chocolate. I followed to ask a few questions and get warm myself.

"Bonnie, if you could address the World Economic Forum, what would you tell them about why you are demonstrating?"

"I'm standing up for the poor. We have to be brave and not be afraid to stand up and say this is wrong."

"What did you accomplish by demonstrating?"

"I don't know if I accomplished anything, but I live in a free country where I can do this and if I stayed home in my warm bed this morning I'd feel even worse. At least I tried."

"Janet, how would you change the present system to help the poor?"

"I don't know that I have an alternative. I just believe the present system doesn't work for the poor."

"What does globalization mean?" I asked Bonnie Phelps.

"Money. Money and power. Whoever has the money has the power."

Phelps and Dorman may speak of globalization in the simplest of terms, but their mere presence—their witness—was sufficient to articulate the deep sense of unease that many people who are far less conversant on the details than Stiglitz and Soros also feel about globalization's consequences. Like Phelps and Dorman, many come by their unease because of deeply ingrained spiritual beliefs that consciously or unconsciously guide their thoughts and, ultimately, their actions.

That sets them apart from secular critics such as Stiglitz and Soros, who find fault with globalization mostly on economic and political grounds, although they may recognize the moral dimension as well. Economics and politics, of course, hold enormous consequences for people. Markets can be forces for good. To function smoothly, markets require political stability. They therefore seek to promote peace and financial growth to heighten consumer confidence and buying power. Globalization's proponents say the greater the degree of globalization in a nation, generally speaking, the greater the degree of political freedom and equality of income distribution.[6] Of course, critics can point to China, one of the world's fastest growing markets, which by any reasonable measure sorely lacks political freedom and which suffers from enormous, and growing, income inequality between its rural and urban areas.[7] They can also note the enormous environmental implications of the global economy's growing demand for natural resources.

As important as economics and politics are to the discussion of globalization, they are not the focus of this book. They matter here only insofar as they impact the inner search for truth we call spirituality and the outer manifestation of that process, which we call religion. My hope is to explore what the great religious traditions say about globalization, and how individuals informed by these traditions are reacting to it. My concerns are values, identity, and salvation. My guides are the likes of Pope John Paul II, who warns:

> Not all forms of ethics are worthy of the name. We are seeing the emergence of patterns of ethical thinking which are by-products of globalization itself and which bear the stamp of utilitarianism.... Ethics demands that systems be attuned to the needs of man, and not that man be sacrificed for the sake of the system.[8]

The religious critique of globalization dwells on the intrinsic value of human life, the natural world, and community, but one does not have to be religious, formally or otherwise, to share those concerns. Religious-based approaches toward globalization also evaluate the process in relation to their vision of salvation—a word that has different meanings for different faiths, but which I use to denote alignment with whatever a tradition says is the final state of human fulfillment. Globalization's secular critics talk about humanizing the process and reforming the markets to level the playing field and enlarge access to the pie. Essentially, they propose a materialist correction in line with a secular worldview.

Religious-based critics take a different approach. They say globalization's essential economic—or material—formulation is the very root of its problems. For them, economics is beside the point. The real issue, they say, is adopting a spiritual perspective—not to the exclusion of the material, but in addition to it. The consideration of globalization requires spiritual vision, believers say, simply because everything in life requires spiritual vision for optimum clarity. To do without that perspective is to ignore life's deepest well.

Religious perspectives differ about important details—sometimes even violently—but strip away the veneer of theology and every spiritual path worth the label teaches that the essence of life is the struggle to discern transcendent meaning from worldly experiences and to try to live in accordance with that understanding. Globalization, then, differs not at all from any other human condition; if its problems are to be satisfactorily addressed, they must be approached in the same spirit as any other condition, say the faithful.

Bonnie Phelps and Janet Dorman, for example, speak as liberal Protestants motivated by a religious tradition that sees social reform as a Christian duty. Their God is a just

God, so they take to the street to further a consciousness conducive to the growth of justice that they, in their moments of strongest faith, believe can transform the injustice they see in the global village.

> The consideration of globalization requires spiritual vision, believers say, simply because everything in life requires spiritual vision for optimum clarity. To do without that perspective is to ignore life's deepest well.

A Buddhist, in contrast, might also conclude that globalization is indeed problematic but would arrive at that end point through a different cognitive process. There is no "God" in the Western sense to demand justice of the Buddhist. But there is the *dharma*, the right path, that demands proper conduct if we are to eradicate *dukkha*, suffering—literally the bane of existence. And since the dharma dictates compassion, generosity, and the stifling of greed, globalization—to the degree that compassion and generosity are missing and greed is endorsed—cannot be in alignment with the Buddhist way and therefore requires a corrective that steers it toward the right path.

A Bahá'í would view globalization still differently. Bahá'ís see in globalization the blueprint of God's ultimate plan, which for them is the unification of human society on every level. For the Bahá'í, the problems associated with globalization are indicative of the present incompleteness of the process of salvation. Over time—how much time is a mystery—human effort will overcome globalization's apparent injustices through reason and fair-mindedness. But make no mistake: human effort must be extended to that end and to bring the individual into alignment with the grand design.

In a world that seems largely secularized, of what importance are the theological beliefs of liberal Protestants, Buddhists, Bahá'ís, or other religious believers? After all, hasn't the market grabbed the pedestal that human society once reserved for its varied concepts of God? All that remains, it would seem, is tinkering with globalization's frayed edges to keep those made angry and dangerous by being on the losing end of the process from seeking their revenge. Reflecting this attitude following the World Trade Center attack, Robert Wright, a renowned champion of globalization, wrote:

> If it turns out that a bleeding-heart concern for the plight of the poor and alienated Muslims around the world would help quell terrorism, global capitalism should in theory embrace that concern…. In sum: The good news is that in order to save the world, we don't have to convince CEOs to think about something other than money. The bad news is that we have to get them to think very long-term—to think about earnings ten, even 20 or 30 years down the road.[9]

How cynical and shortsighted. Wright speaks of Muslims—members of a faith that because of its particular history and internal dynamics is notably antagonistic toward much of what is associated with globalization—as though they were wholly economic beings. His remarks disregard Muslims' widely held sense of injustice suffered at the hands of the West, and their belief that Islam, not the WTO, is God's idea of how globalization should look.

Huston Smith, the preeminent scholar of comparative religion, notes that before the claims of science won out, we all shared what he calls a "traditional" worldview—that is, people everywhere based their actions on conclusions reached by interpreting the world through the prism of their culture's religious beliefs, regardless of whether they called themselves Muslims, Christians, Hindus, or something else. And despite all appearances to the contrary, those many centuries of inner conditioning remain with us and still direct us—Smith would say that is because something within the human DNA dictates that the traditional view is the truer vision:

> To say that the pilgrim is not alone in her heroic journey understates the case, for it is the spark of divinity that God plants in human beings that initiates the journey in the first place. Transcendence takes the initiative at every turn: in creating the world, in instantiating itself in human beings, and in shaping civilizations through its revelations— revelations that set civilizations in motion and establish their trajectories.[10]

I take no position here on the veracity of any particular religious beliefs or spiritual path. My effort is only to explain the beliefs in relation to globalization. However, I agree strongly with Smith that humans are programmed to search the inner cosmos for meaning and that recent world events underscore how important their religious conclusions

are to actions taken. Understanding how these beliefs moti-
vate individuals is crucial if we are to cope successfully
with the stresses that threaten to blow our world apart, and
which seem only aggravated by globalization.

Despite the liberal sampling of other faiths and practices that has taken hold among many in the United States
and other Western nations, it is the more traditional forms
of belief that appear on the rise worldwide, to a degree that
religious scholars of a few decades back dismissed as
improbable. Evangelical and Pentecostal Protestant
Christianity in America and Africa, a resurgent Islam,
India's Hindu revival, the return to traditional practice in
Judaism—all these are examples of the grip that the major
traditions maintain over so many.

This book looks at the beliefs of eight religious traditions that shape the attitudes of followers as they confront
globalization. Also considered is how globalization has
changed the way the traditions function in the world. As
with everything, globalization is a process of give and take.

The eight traditions are the Bahá'í Faith, Buddhism,
Hinduism, Islam, Judaism, Protestantism, Roman Catholicism, and what I have called Tribal and Earth-based
Religions. The latter includes both indigenous and neo-
pagan traditions, which despite their seemingly vast differences are no more dissimilar than many Protestant
denominations are from each other. Together, these
traditions account for most of the world's population
(China's Confucian culture being the notable exception).

One, the Bahá'í Faith, comes closest in its founding
theology to addressing the particulars of contemporary

globalization. Some see salvation as the world coming around to their view—it's not globalization they oppose, it's just a question of whose globalization will prevail. However, each offers guiding principles for dealing with the decisions individuals make in their economic and communal lives. And in each case, a core principle conflicts with globalization's embrace of what the Buddhist scholar David Loy has called "moneytheism."[11]

Globalization presents an extraordinary challenge. You may think it a positive or a negative. You may believe that globalization just needs a course correction to make it more "fair" or think that it requires a fundamental overhaul to save humanity's "soul." But rest assured that globalization is a phenomenon that is radically changing human society, and quite likely the "society" of every other life-form with which we share the planet. Like the proverbial scrambled egg, there's no putting things back the way they were. All we can do is try and understand it.

> We cannot live in a world in which our economies and markets are global, our political awareness is global, our business relationships take us to every continent, and the Internet connects us with colleagues half a world away and yet live on Friday, or Saturday, or Sunday with ideas of God that are essentially provincial, imagining that somehow the one we call God has been primarily concerned with us and our tribe.[12]

Harvard University religion scholar Diana L. Eck wrote those words as a plea for interfaith understanding in what has become the world's most religiously pluralistic nation, the United States. That fact is a byproduct of globalization and as good a reason as any to seek understanding of what the world's traditions make of it all. Because when Pope John Paul II, evangelical television entrepreneur Pat Robertson, the National Council of Churches of Christ, the Union of American Hebrew Congregations, Buddhist groups, Muslims, Hindus, Wiccans, Bahá'ís, and others all embrace debt relief for the world's poorest nations unable to meet the challenge of globalization, something important is building. Bonnie Phelps and Janet Dorman understand that.

1

Roman Catholicism:
SOLIDARITY IN JUSTICE

ROBERT WALDROP IS A BEAR OF A MAN, a 260-pound six-footer
with a flowing beard and an opinion on everything, including a favorite Bible passage—which is, "He who trusts in
the Lord shall be made fat." As Waldrop says, "it's in there
somewhere." Yes, the man is a jokester, and quick to share
a good laugh. But Waldrop is serious about applying his
understanding of Roman Catholic teachings to daily living.[1] Those teachings, he says, may be reduced to a simple
statement: "Noncooperation with evil, cooperation with
virtue." As far as Waldrop is concerned, the prevailing economic order falls squarely into the former category.

> Whenever possible, I spend my dollars at locally
> owned and operated businesses, preferring inde-
> pendents to franchises, and a union label is a plus.
> I never go to the big fast food places—McDonald's,
> Burger King, et cetera. If I want a hamburger, I go

to a local independent who is capable of making a burger without being supervised by a transnational corporation. I put my retirement fund that I have through the archdiocese in the bond and cash fund, rather than the stock fund, to avoid such entanglements.

More than most, the fifty-year-old Waldrop walks his talk. He's a committed member of the Catholic Worker movement (started by the legendary Catholic social reformers Dorothy Day and Peter Maurin), living in Oklahoma City, where he shares an eighty-year-old house near downtown with other group members, five cats, and two dogs. He's turned his front lawn into an organic vegetable garden, he runs a home delivery food pantry for people who can't normally get to such outlets (elderly shut-ins, single moms with no transportation), drives a 1989 Chevy pickup, and makes ends meet by working thirty hours a week as music director for one of Oklahoma City's wealthiest parishes ("It's also important to help the rich connect to the poor," he says). He also edits an irregularly published local version of the *Catholic Worker* newspaper and produces a host of regularly updated Web sites he estimates contain over one million pages of content. Some of the pages offer useful tips for surviving on little money. A lot more pages offer material he's written or collected from elsewhere relating to Catholic social teachings, particularly economic justice and its application to globalization. Says Waldrop:

Globalization, in terms of the reduction of legal barriers that separate peoples and also in terms of developing solidarity among the various peoples of the world, is, as the Holy Father has often noted, a good thing. But the globalization of exploitation and "robbing the poor to pay the rich" is a very bad thing. Indeed, this is killing the poor and driving many of the poorest of the poor to the point of desperation.

Roman Catholic teachings are a distinct blend of doctrines often viewed by outsiders as conservative on lifestyle issues and liberal on social welfare issues. A committed Catholic might put it differently, however. He or she might say it's simply a matter of advocating a consistent ethic of life, of adhering to the belief that consistency is a hallmark of the moral life. Think of it as a seamless garment that both smothers evil and shelters virtue. "You can't campaign against abortion and not also be against violence against women. You can't be against abortion and for capital punishment. You can't be against war while ignoring economic exploitation, because those exploited will eventually react violently to continued exploitation. You can't be ambiguous and call yourself a moral being," says Waldrop.

When it comes to massive, top-down bureaucratic structures, the Catholic Church sets the gold standard among the world's major faiths. From pope to parish, the world's estimated one billion Roman Catholics live, at least theoretically, within a global, hierarchical system that relies on scripture and tradition to stake its claim as *the* One True Church: the universal, uninterrupted, and transcendent successor to the nascent Christian church established by St. Peter the Apostle. An examination of Catholic attitudes toward globalization, therefore, requires starting at the top, with the person of the Holy Father, Pope John Paul II.

The pontificate of Karol Józef Wojtyła has been among the longest in church history and extraordinarily prolific. As Pope John Paul II, he has traveled more widely, addressed more people, created more saints, and issued more encyclicals and other papal documents than any of his 262 predecessors. He has reached out to other faiths and injected himself and his church into world events, becoming an unequalled moral force and—thanks to the globalization of communications—history's first pop celebrity pope.

"John Paul II radically recast the papacy for the twenty-first century and the third millennium by returning the Office of Peter to its evangelical roots," wrote the pope's biographer, George Weigel. "The world and the Church no longer think of the pope as the chief executive officer of the Roman Catholic Church; the world and the Church experience the pope as pastor, an evangelist, and a witness."[2]

Through it all, John Paul has displayed a consistency that Waldrop seeks in his own life. The pope has stressed traditional values in connection with family life issues such as marriage, contraception, and divorce; and historic doctrine in connection with issues such as hierarchical authority, priestly celibacy, and women's ordination. Some would say he has been too stringent in his adherence to the past, too authoritarian, too rigid, and too unwilling to share power with the bishops and laity that his critics say was mandated by the church's great liberalizing event, the 1960s' Second Vatican Council. These critics would also say

John Paul has undermined church authority by sticking to uncompromising positions despite the widespread rejection of his opposition to abortion, birth control, premarital sex, and other personal morality dictates by modernist lay Catholics, particularly in North America and Western Europe. Some would even indirectly blame the priestly sex scandals that have rocked the United States church, as well as those of Ireland, Poland, Germany, and elsewhere, on his intransigence on the questions of priestly celibacy and women's ordination.

One of John Paul's harshest critics, Hans Küng, a dissident Catholic theologian whose rejection of papal infallibility and other key Catholic beliefs prompted the revocation of his ability to teach Catholic theology at Germany's University of Tübingen, says the pope displays a "zealous anti-modernism" and "rigorous moralism" that seeks to split society into "sponsors of life and conspirators against life."[3]

Robert J. Schreiter, a priest and professor of doctrinal theology at Chicago's Catholic Theological Union, explains some of the pope's actions as a direct response to globalization, in particular the process of cultural liberalization it has engendered. He labels it a case of revanchism, an attempt to regain ground lost to globalization's tendency to decentralize power by creating horizontal rather than vertical lines of communication (consider the free-wheeling Internet's democratization of information and affinity-group discussions). "Revanchism," he says, "is what would appear to be part of the policy of the latter part of the pontificate of John Paul II."

An example of this, says Schreiter, is the pope's record of appointing bishops who are "unswervingly loyal to the Vatican" regardless of the wishes of local Catholics. "The power of episcopal [bishop] conferences and anything that would diminish the centralized power of the Vatican is called into question.... There seems to be little trust in what is emerging as globalized means of communication. Hierarchical means are reasserted." The point, Schreiter adds, is to maintain a "selective engagement" with globalization "that tries to capture control of the leadership of globalizing trends and direct them in a certain way."[4]

Papal critics, both harsh and mild, abound. But the larger debate over the rightness of John Paul's policies is for others to thrash out. My concern here is restricted to the pope's social teachings, because in them may be found the core of Catholicism's nuanced approach toward globalization's economic and cultural repercussions.

The first non-Italian pope in 450 years, John Paul has been steady in his defense of democracy and capitalism, both of which globalization proponents say are requisite for the success of the process, and which he, a man who experienced both Nazi and Soviet totalitarianism, regards as the best political and economic systems for nurturing the human spirit. But the pope is no supporter of unbridled freedom or unrestricted free markets. His criticism of libertarian individualism has been obvious. The same holds true for his attacks on capitalism's rapacious tendencies. During his historic 1998 visit to communist Cuba, for example, the pope delighted Fidel Castro, Marxism's last icon, by criticizing "neoliberal" capitalism that "subordinates the human person to blind market forces and conditions the development of people on those forces."[5] The comment, made at an open-air Mass before some three hundred thousand Cubans gathered in Havana's Plaza of the Revolution, should be placed in the context of the pope's equally sharp criticism of repressive political systems, including the one run by Castro. Nonetheless, it underscores the sharp distinction between the church of John Paul and globalization's laissez-faire advocates.

On the first day of the new millennium, a day designated as a World Day of Peace by the church, John Paul spoke of war as a "defeat for humanity," its cause rooted in "a logic of supremacy fuelled by the desire to dominate and exploit others, by ideologies of power or totalitarian utopias, by crazed nationalisms or tribal hatred." He went on to praise those who work for peace, the advances of science and technology that make it possible "to overcome dreadful diseases and to enhance and prolong human life." However,

In Pope John Paul II's social teachings may be found the core of Catholicism's approach toward globalization's economic and cultural repercussions.

- The church is universal in outlook and welcomes globalization's promise of bringing people together
- Economic growth must be fair to all, in particular to those most lacking the ability to compete in a globalized world
- The practice of putting corporate profits at a higher priority than the dignity and justice of workers is morally inadmissible
- The creation of community promotes peace and spiritual wholeness for humanity

he added, peace will only result when "humanity as a whole rediscovers its fundamental calling to be one family, a family in which the dignity and rights of individuals— whatever their status, race, or religion—are accepted as prior and superior to any kind of difference or distinction."

Globalization, "for all its risks," offers the promise of achieving the church's vision of a single human family "built on the values of justice, equality and solidarity," he continued. But economic justice must be considered, particularly

> in the principle of the universal destination of the earth's resources. This principle does not delegitimize private property; instead it broadens the understanding and management of private property to embrace its indispensable social function, to the advantage of the common good and in particular the good of society's weakest members.... Perhaps the time has come for a new and deeper reflection on the nature of the economy and its purpose. What seems to be urgently needed is a reconsideration of the concept of "prosperity" itself, to prevent it from being enclosed in a narrow utilitarian perspective which leaves very little space for values such as solidarity and altruism.... An economy which takes no account of the ethical dimension and does not seek to serve the good of the person—of every person and the whole person— cannot really call itself an "economy," understood in the sense of a rational and constructive use of material wealth.[6]

John Paul's remarks, delivered on January 1, 2000, make clear his views on globalization, which can be restated as follows. The Catholic Church is universal in outlook and practice and as such welcomes globalization's promises of bringing people together. However, globalization's application is deeply flawed because economic prowess is not enough. Rather, economic growth must be fair to all, in particular those most lacking the ability to compete. This is the meaning of human dignity and justice. This is what creates community. This is what promotes peace. This is what enables spiritual wholeness for humanity. This is the teaching of Jesus Christ.

As clear as the World Day of Peace message was, however, it broke little new ground. Instead, it built on previous papal statements made over the course of two decades. Three papal encyclicals in particular set the stage. In the earliest of them, 1981's *Laborem Exercens* (On Human Work), John Paul spoke of workers' dignity, the importance of work to family formation, the "priority of labor over capital," and the rising demands for a voice in "international decision-making" by the world's poor, which "will very probably involve a reduction or a less rapid increase in material well-being for the more developed countries."[7]

In his 1987 encyclical *Sollicitudo Rei Socialis* (On Social Concerns), he spoke of workers' issues depending "more and more on the influence of factors beyond regional boundaries and national frontiers," the "unequal distribution of the means of subsistence originally meant for everybody," the "radical dissatisfaction" resulting from "blind submission to pure consumerism," and the need to reform international trade and world financial systems, which "frequently" discriminate against developing nations while exacerbating their foreign debt problems. He also noted the Catholic "option or love of preference for the poor...to which the whole tradition of the Church bears witness."[8]

And in 1991, in *Centesimus Annus* (On the Hundredth Anniversary of *Rerum Novarum*), which came a century after Pope Leo XIII's groundbreaking encyclical on Catholic social doctrine (which first set the church on its course of opposition to socialism and communism), John Paul commented on the "morally inadmissible" practice of putting corporate profits before people, the "irrational destruction of the natural environment," and the "growing feeling" that the "increasing internationalization of the economy ought to be accompanied by effective international agencies which will oversee and direct the economy to the common good.... Much remains to be done in this area." Once again, John Paul stated the church's "preferential option for the poor" and insisted that "the social message of the Gospel must not be considered a theory, but above all else a basis and motivation for action."[9]

The pope has been unequivocal. Church social doctrine is unequivocal. Nor have the bishops, the pope's appointed representatives, been silent on the matter. Speaking in Paraná, Argentina, in 1999, Cardinal Francis George, archbishop of Chicago, said of globalization:

> These are the values which have attracted the most attention from critics: namely, the search for eco-

nomic profit as the highest human goal and the definition of the human being as a consumer. If profit alone—and especially short-term profit—is seen as the value which organizes an economic system, then human beings and human societies are bound to suffer. Likewise, to value human beings primarily in the light of how much they can consume represents an unacceptable diminution of the dignity of the human person. It is an affront to a basic principle of theological anthropology, namely, that we are created in the image and likeness of God.[10]

American bishops, of course, are by no means the only ones expressing concerns. Philippine bishops have dismissed globalization "based on decisions of a few mega-institutions" and concerned with the "welfare of the powerful and the affluent few" as "the kind of globalization the great majority of humanity would be better without." Canada's bishops have called for a rewriting of sections of the North American Free Trade Agreement that limit the power of national governments to protect the environment from foreign corporate exploitation.[11]

But how has the institutional church, in its broadest sense, responded to all that the pope and bishops have said about globalization? How have individual Catholics responded to the exhortations from their church leaders to resist globalization's negative aspects and, not incidentally, to change the way the most privileged of them live?

Until the demise in 1870 of the Papal States, which existed in what is now Italy, the Roman Catholic Church was indeed a nation unto itself. Today, of course, there is Vatican

City, a ministate among ministates consisting, in the main, of an immense plaza, St. Peter's Basilica, museums, offices, residences, and tourist facilities. In all, it is the world's smallest "independent" state, equal in size to about three-quarters of the National Mall in Washington, D.C. Nonetheless, it has a recognized if limited diplomatic presence at the United Nations, the European Union, and other such transnational bodies—and far more political clout than nations many times larger.

Weigel, the papal biographer, maintains that it was the loss of primary temporal power that allowed the church to transform itself into "a universal moral reference point" and the pope into a "global witness."[12] Again, there are many who would disagree with Weigel's characterizations, and they might cite the church's vast wealth as being in conflict with its teachings about aiding the poor, as well as its opposition to what the critics would consider important advances in—to cite one issue—world population control, which the church has helped block at international forums. Thomas Berry, the Catholic monk, "eco-theologian," and social thinker, faults the church—as he does most faith groups—for still putting too much emphasis on the holiness of a church interior and priest over the "holiness" of nature, family, and friends.[13] And then there's Küng. He blames the pope, among many other things, for *causing* rather than stopping abortion by opposing population curbs. That stand, in Küng's view, leads to unwanted pregnancies and encourages additional abortions.[14]

The church is slow to change—far too slow for the likes of Berry and Küng. However, as the Reverend Kenneth

Himes has noted, the Catholic Church is an inherently conservative institution that is, in the main, reactive rather
than proactive. Himes, a Franciscan father and moral theologian at Washington Theological Union, points out that
church social teachings, which trace their modern evolution to Pope Leo XIII's 1891 encyclical, have developed over
time in response to changing world conditions. "By that I
mean it is occasional writing written in response to some
event or emerging trend, and it is an effort by pastoral leaders to make sense of the world in which they live from the
perspective of their faith," he says. Leo's encyclical *Rerum
Novarum* (Of New Things) was issued in response to the
emergence of industrial capitalism and its attendant social
disruption and economic inequalities. Now, says Himes,
John Paul and his bishops have, at their own deliberate
pace, picked up the ball in relation to globalization.

The essence of Catholic social doctrine is its emphasis
on the dignity of all people and the belief that full dignity
can only be realized in community. Church social teachings
are an attempt to instruct the faithful about the implications of "these two anthropological claims." But as Himes
says:

> Those implications were not discovered all at
> once.... The teaching has developed over time
> because like all humans and all human enterpris-
> es, it is marked by historicity.... There was a time
> when Catholic teaching was more tolerant of sig-
> nificant inequalities in economic or political life
> as long as the basic moral and religious equality of
> persons was affirmed. Over time we have come to

understand that significant political or economic inequities pose obstacles to the experience and expression of moral and religious equality.

Echoing John Paul, Himes says that the next phase of globalization must include calls for regulation and oversight of transnational corporations and the international markets in which they operate, and that it must be done in accordance with "a staple of Catholic political theory that the purpose of the state is to promote the common good of society." Catholic social teaching is supportive of efforts to regulate the developing global order. "In this the church's teaching will be at odds with those who equate globalization with an unfettered market system of economics," Himes says.[15]

Himes's point is that the world is changing so rapidly under globalization that it is a struggle for a behemoth of faith such as the Roman Catholic Church just to maintain rhetorical pace with the altered landscape. However, the church already is a globalized entity; "catholic" with a small "c" does, after all, mean "universal." Powerful and effective mechanisms are already in place and working to mitigate globalization's more onerous repercussions. "The advantage of the Catholic Church is that it is truly global," says Sister Judy Cannon, associate director for Social Mission of the Leadership Conference of Women Religious, a church-sanctioned organization for Catholic sisters. "It has members and leaders all over the world, is able to get information for everywhere and has experience everywhere. That enables the church to be more sensitive."

Catholic religious orders are one example of the church's global reach. Mother Teresa, the nun whose dedication to the poorest of the poor earned her the well-deserved name Saint of the Gutters, created the Missionaries of Charity, an order of nuns that spread from India to the inner cities of the United States and other Western nations—a reminder that modern church institutions have also been changed by globalization's two-way street. Mother Teresa put her devotion to the Gospel into daily action by giving love and sustenance to society's most downtrodden. She did not, however, directly challenge the elite institutions and nations profiting most from globalization. The Maryknoll orders of sisters, brothers, and priests do.

Working around the globe, Maryknoll men and women advocate, organize, and educate on "peace, social justice and the integrity of the creation," as the motto of the movement's Office of Global Concerns states. Maryknoll representatives may be found lobbying the United Nations, national governments, international financial institutions, and the corporate world on behalf

The Roman Catholic Church itself is a globalized entity. Powerful and effective mechanisms are already in place and working to mitigate globalization's negative effects and to promote the common good of society. They include the pope's moral authority; the bishops who act on his behalf around the world; the international orders of brothers, priests, sisters, and nuns; the worldwide aid and development agency Caritas Internationalis; and the grassroots commitments of dedicated laypeople.

Working in tandem, they present a formidable front for advancing Catholic social teachings that stands in opposition to many of the values promulgated by globalization.

of refugees, AIDS sufferers, orphans, and others. Maryknoll also runs an affiliates program for lay Catholics who support the broader movement. More than fifty local affiliate chapters exist in the United States and Puerto Rico, in addition to others in such nations as Peru, the Philippines, and Nicaragua. The basis for all Maryknoll cross-cultural mission work is church social teaching, notes Marie Dennis, who heads the Maryknoll Office for Global Concerns in Washington, D.C.

"The church has a really strong base of social teaching upon which to draw," she says. "Do we need to move faster? Of course. There is so much to be done. But the basic theology and the basic teaching are there. That gives the church the capacity to at least say there is a problem, and it says that pretty well.... There are a number of Catholic religious communities that have put a great deal of energy into trying to understand the impact of globalization, and I would say the level of sophistication about the issue is phenomenal. That's a good and important first step."

Another example of the church's global reach is its century-old aid and development agency, Caritas Internationalis. A Vatican-based confederation of 154 Catholic relief, development, and social service organizations working in almost two hundred nations and territories, Caritas operates as well as it does because of the global Catholic network and the feedback and connections that produces. Consequently, Caritas officials have long been cognizant of globalization's implications and involved in trying to offset the harm to the powerless and the environment that it sees constantly arising.

Caritas works at a grassroots level in development, conflict resolution, and disaster relief. It also lobbies governments and international institutions in an effort to enable the poor to become "active collaborators in the pursuit of justice rather than mere passive recipients."[16] In the United States, Baltimore-based Catholic Relief Services (CRS) is the Caritas affiliate and, in fact, is Caritas's largest national participant, with an annual budget of about 370 million dollars and projects in eighty nations. Ian Gary is CRS's strategic issues adviser for Africa. His assessment of CRS's involvement in an oil pipeline project in Chad and Cameroon is a clear example of how church institutions leverage their networking abilities and moral influence on a global level.

The 3.7-billion-dollar Chad-Cameroon pipeline project involves three international petroleum companies, the World Bank, and the governments of Chad and Cameroon. Its aim is to send oil extracted in Chad to Cameroon, from which it will be exported to the world market. However, soon after the project was announced, concerns were raised locally about the project's environmental consequences, compensation for relocated peoples, jobs for locals, and whether government corruption and repression would preclude those nations' ordinary citizens from reaping any benefit from the endeavor. In an effort to ameliorate those concerns, CRS began working with local Catholic officials, providing financial support, information on the project, and strategic advice on how to deal with pipeline advocates and officials. In October 1999, Cameroon Catholic and Protestant officials issued a joint statement outlining their concerns. The United States

Conference of Catholic Bishops, the organizational umbrella for the American church hierarchy, then brought the statement to the attention of World Bank and U.S. Treasury officials in Washington. It also brought the secretary-general of the Catholic Conference of Cameroon to the United States for meetings with officials from those two agencies, as well as other international finance, U.S. government, and oil company representatives. The Cameroon church leader, Father Patrick Lafon, also spoke with the *Wall Street Journal* and other media, and briefed the Interfaith Center on Corporate Responsibility, which presented a shareholders resolution on the project at ExxonMobil's annual meeting.[17]

The results were changes in design and routing to avoid some of the most environmentally sensitive areas and increased compensation rates for locals. The attention also prompted the World Bank to establish an independent advisory group to keep tabs on the project. Gary said CRS remains involved, monitoring the pipeline's progress and dealing with the myriad of problems that arise. "This is what we do. We stay with it and keep plugging away on behalf of the people most impacted," he says. "We may not get everything we want, but we plug away so that the genuine needs of people and the land are not ignored."

Then there is the power of the papal bull pulpit. A prime example of John Paul's ability to move the international community was his role in the Jubilee 2000 campaign.

Since the 1980s, John Paul had been urging cancellation of the massive international debt—made worse each year by the process of compound interest—that burdens those poorest nations least able to repay international banks and lending agencies, and forces them to divert limited resources from health, education, and other desperately needed domestic projects to debt servicing. A decade later, the idea seized the public's imagination and resulted in the promise of billions of dollars of relief by lender states and agencies. The effort's success was due in large measure to the work of thousands of activist non-Catholics as well as Catholics, and some prominent rock stars and other celebrities (U2's Bono called the pope a "funky pontiff" following a meeting with him on the Jubilee 2000 campaign).[18] Undeniably, though, it was the pope's support—his visibility and moral weight—that gave the effort the extra push it needed to move governments and bankers to action. Debt relief, said John Paul, "is, in many ways, a precondition for the poorest countries to make progress in their fight against poverty."[19]

Church institutions—the pope, the bishops, Caritas, Maryknoll, and others—continue to press for additional strides in relieving the crushing debt burden, a result in many cases of pressure on poor countries to borrow as a way into the global economy but which often leads to waste and theft as a result of government corruption and incompetence. Debt reduction also continues to resonate on a more grassroots Catholic level. "There's been a pretty good echo of this on the parish level," says Maryknoll's Dennis. "It's spoken about often; it's a chance for people to understand what's going on, on a global level."

The Catholic Church regards globalization's cultural message to be inherently secular: goods and property are what count, not God and spirit. However, globalization has

also presented the church with a problem of religious competition in Latin America, Africa, and elsewhere. The contemporary ease of global communication systems and
travel has enabled American and European evangelical and
Pentecostal Protestant groups to make substantial inroads
in previously Catholic-dominated regions. The shortage of
priests—who because of their unique status are key to
Catholic practice and parish life—in North America and
Europe is well documented. Receiving less attention is the
more severe shortage in the developing world, a big reason
why the Protestant groups have fared as well as they have.

Europe and North America presently account for 35
percent of Catholic believers and 68 percent of all priests,
says Philip Jenkins, a professor of religion at Pennsylvania
State University and author of *The Next Christendom: The
Coming of Global Christianity.* Latin America, with 42 percent of believers, can claim only 20 percent of the priest-
hood's membership. No wonder the church is losing ground,
Jenkins concludes. Africa, where the church has grown
fastest in recent decades, suffers from similar priest shortages. Logically, it stands to reason that a globally focused
institution such as the church would export priests from
Europe and North America to ease some of the shortage in
Latin America and Africa. However, that's an "inconceiv-
able" prospect, says Jenkins. European and North American
dioceses are not about to worsen their own situations. Still,
what has happened befuddles him.

Amazingly enough, the main steps taken so far to
remedy priest shortages have been entirely in the

opposite direction, namely in importing Third
World priests in order to meet shortfalls in North
America and Europe. Viewed in a global perspective, such a policy can be described at best as
painfully short sighted, at worst as suicidal for
Catholic fortunes. If even an organization as centralized and as globally minded as the Catholic
Church cannot mobilize its resources to meet the
emerging challenges and opportunities of the global South, what hope is there for any other body?[20]

The challenges of globalization are legion. Jobs disappear as capital is moved overseas. The increased movement
of people across borders is changing long-held concepts
about national identity. Global media make distant problems an immediate concern. If the church hierarchy and
institutions struggle with it, what's the ordinary Catholic to
do? Francis X. Maier, chancellor of the Archdiocese of
Denver, advises people to first get educated about the
world. "Most Catholics don't think very deeply about globalization," he says, despite the church's efforts around debt
relief lauded by Dennis.

One Catholic who does think deeply about globalization is Father Tissa Balasuriya. A Sri Lankan who was
excommunicated by the Vatican for a year in the late 1990s
because of his perceived denial of such basic church doctrines as original sin and Jesus' divinity, he thinks ordinary
Catholics need to do much more than just reflect on the
issue. Balasuriya, reflecting a widespread sentiment among
non-Western theologians, Catholic and otherwise, says

Westerners have been the main proponents and beneficiaries of globalization. Therefore, Westerners in particular must take greater responsibility for the problems of globalization. What is needed, he says, is "advocacy of global responsibility of those who have accumulated capital and resources for sharing and global transformation."[21]

But other Catholics who also think deeply about globalization say that for all its faults, it still offers the world's poor their best hope, and that this must not be overlooked by those quick to criticize the process for their own alleged political reasons.

The Catholic Church is, after all, a very large tent. Contradictory opinions abound. When forty Italian Catholic groups aligned themselves with anti-globalization protestors at the Genoa G-8 summit (the group of leading industrialized nations) in 2001, some thirty other Italian Catholic intellectuals, journalists, and scientists released a document taking the groups to task for what they argued was a failure to uphold church values. Their pro–free-market document—which linked the anti-globalization side to the left-leaning liberation theologies promul-

> A widespread sentiment among non-Western Catholics says that Westerners have been the main proponents and beneficiaries of globalization, and therefore Westerners in particular must take greater responsibility for the problems of globalization. But other Catholics who also think deeply about globalization say that for all its faults, it still offers the world's poor their best hope, and that this must not be overlooked by those quick to criticize the process for their own alleged political reasons.

gated largely by non-Western Catholics and thoroughly rejected by John Paul—maintained that "countries that are open to trade have greater growth than those that are not." Anti-globalization activists, it continued, "demonize development, technology and science" and display "contempt for human reason."[22]

Writing in *First Things*, the Reverend Richard John Neuhaus, editor in chief of the monthly magazine, castigated anti-globalists for exhibiting "a desire to exclude poor nations from what the encyclical *Centesimus Annus* calls the circle of productivity and exchange." In another edition of the same publication, Neuhaus, a prominent American Catholic conservative, wrote that globalization "has become a synonym for capitalism in some circles, including Christians not yet weaned from the excitements of Marxist class struggle." Again pointing to *Centesimus Annus*, Neuhaus added:

> What the Church does is bear witness both to the creative capacities of man in producing wealth *and* to the imperative that creativity be exercised in a way that respects the absolute dignity of persons and is aimed at including everyone "in the circle of productivity and exchange." Those who dismiss such witness as mere moralizing are in fact declaring their inability or unwillingness to respond to moral truth.[23]

Back in Oklahoma City, Robert Waldrop quotes the same papal encyclicals, the same social teachings, the same option for the poor—yet disagrees mightily with Neuhaus's conclusions on *how* to achieve a just social contract. But both men are fully committed to the Catholic Church, to the social teaching, to the leadership of Pope John Paul II. They have no disagreement over *whether* a just social contract is the goal, only about how best to get there. In a catholic church, such diversity is to be expected. In the Catholic Church, that open debate over how to understand globalization and maximize its promise may be the best guide for ordinary Catholics seeking the same.

2

Islam:
GOD AS HISTORY

IN LATE 2001, after U.S.-led coalition forces routed the Taliban, Sayyid M. Syeed received a telephone call from a newspaper reporter. A CNN talk show had linked up American and Afghan teenagers via satellite and asked them to comment on a photograph of the enticingly dressed singer and actress Jennifer Lopez, known to her fans as "J.Lo." The point was to underscore the vast differences between American and Afghan culture. Almost on cue, the Afghan teens reacted negatively. J.Lo's minimalist dress code offended their deeply conservative Muslim values. The Americans, of course, said no big deal. Now the newspaper reporter wanted a comment from Syeed, who as secretary-general of the Indiana-based Islamic Society of North America, is an often-quoted Muslim voice in American media. What, he was asked, did the made-for-TV exchange say about the ability of the two cultures to get along?

"I said, 'It was provocation. Why show Jennifer Lopez? She doesn't represent all of America. I live in America! I don't go to see Jennifer Lopez! Why use her as the baseline? Our gift to Afghanistan should be what is best about America, its tolerance, its democracy. What about positive values, not some barely dressed pop star? Why not ask Afghan teenagers how they feel about the good things? The answer will be very different.'"

The next day the newspaper ran a story featuring Syeed's comments beneath a headline that implied criticism of Lopez by him. "They said I fumed at her," Syeed recalls. It was enough to produce scores of angry telephone calls and e-mails from Lopez fans. "I asked people in my office, 'What did I do?' Don't they understand that people elsewhere in the world, that Muslims, can think differently?"

No major religious community has reacted with the same degree of negativity to the rapid spread of cultural and economic globalization as the world's Muslims. Surely, no religious community is perceived in the West—globalization's font—as being anywhere near as hostile to the values touted by free-market transnational economics and the spread of J.Lo culture as Islam. Bloody attacks by terrorists claiming to act on behalf of Islam—and who blame the West for the myriad and complex economic, social, and political problems found in Muslim nations—provide ample evidence for the perception.

But it is not that Islam is adverse to the rise of one system for all the world's people. Islam is not anti-globalization. It is far from it. Rather, Islam is *alter*-globalization.[1]

Islam views itself as the concluding revelation of the tripartite Abrahamic monotheistic tradition, a corrective to the misunderstandings Muslims say limited Judaism and Christianity. Judaism's limitation was its tribal orientation. Christianity's was its deviation from strict monotheism by adoption of the Trinity. Islam, Muslims believe, reconstituted the pure religion of the prophet Abraham, the path intended by God—Allah, as Muslims would say—for all humanity.

So when anti-Western Muslims rile against globalization, what they mean is they oppose a system that is not rooted in Islam. The difference is profound. The form of globalization they reject is one that elevates the free market above all else, including cultural and ethical "encumbrances."[2] The globalization they favor is Islamic, a system that offers "a holistic approach to human society in which economic growth and material advancement [are] only the means to the end and not the end in itself," says Ameer Ali, an economics professor at the University of Western Australia specializing in Muslim development issues.[3] The Qur'an—Islam's scriptural text that tradition-minded Muslims regard as the literal word of God, and which occupies a place in Islam akin to that of Jesus in the traditional Christian paradigm—makes clear the faith's global mission: "Verily, this is no less than a message to all the worlds" (81:27).

"Globalization would be great if done right, if it were just," says Hatem Bazian, an Islamic scholar at the University of California at Berkeley.

It's not that everyone has to become a Muslim, but there are certain Islamic values that are also universal, that every religion recognizes as consistent with righteous living. No religion says greed is good, for example. Fair and equitable treatment is the ethical norm among religions, and of course for Islam. The globalization of righteous values is inherently Islamic, and is what the world needs. Globalism is God's plan. The Qur'an even says that we have been created as various "nations and tribes that ye may know each other, not that ye may despise each other."

Islam was born in seventh-century Arabia, a place of constantly warring tribes, flourishing trade, and a hierarchy of gods. That status quo was challenged one night in 610 C.E., when a successful caravan leader named Muhammad ibn Abdallah, praying in a cave on Mount Hira outside Mecca, received what he later said was a divine revelation, the first of 114 that became the chapters, or *surahs*, of the Qur'an (the "recitation"). God had become text. Muhammad the trader was now the Prophet Muhammad, the Messenger of God. The world would be forever changed.

Spiritual insight becomes orthodox religion, and religion becomes cultural standard. But none of this happens without general upheaval, and this is what began to unfold for the Prophet and Arabia when, two years after receiving the first revelation, Muhammad began to preach publicly and gather followers. The first to follow was his wife, Khadija. Islam ("surrender") had come into being. A Muslim was one who surrendered to God and faith.

Early Muslim history is epic and worthy of its own volume (certainly many have been produced). For us, the narrative is important because of its relation to the Muslim sense of history that in large part explains Islam's reaction to Western-led globalization. But rather than getting bogged down in the details of that history, let's consider it in an admittedly bare-bones fashion.

After his teachings gained attention, Muhammad and his growing band of Muslims came into conflict with Mecca's established polytheistic order. But the city of Yathrib (now called Medina) beckoned in the form of an offer for Muhammad to take over the leadership of that community. Battles raged, and Muhammad's fortunes ebbed and flowed. Yet by the time of his death in 632, he was the most powerful person in Arabia and Islam's survival was assured. A century later—thanks to conquest, commerce, and conversion—Islam stretched from the Atlantic Ocean to China, from sub-Saharan Africa to Southern Europe. It had all become *dar al-Islam*, "the House of Islam." Islam was now perched on the edge of its Golden Age. Islamic ideas flourished. Here's the eminent scholar of comparative religion Huston Smith describing what happened:

> The development of a fabulous culture, the rise of literature, science, medicine, art and architecture; the glory of Damascus, Baghdad and Egypt, and the splendor of Spain under the Moors.... The story of how during Europe's Dark Ages Muslim philosophers and scientists kept the lamp of learning kindled, ready to spark the Western mind when it roused from its long sleep.[4]

The globalization of Islam continued. India, the Indonesian archipelago, and the Balkans came under

Islam's influence. Over the centuries the Muslim world expanded and receded along its edges. Muslim dynasties came and went. And then came decline, colonization by the European powers, economic stagnation, and cultural inertia, followed in the post-colonial era by Western political and cultural hegemony. Islam—the professed faith today of well over one billion people and the world's second largest religion—found itself on the losing end of history, consigned to a subservient role.

But how could that happen if Islam is truly Allah's final revelation? What would acceptance of diminished status say about the belief in an all-powerful God? The only acceptable answer for devout Muslims is belief in Islam's eventual triumph. This is why history and world events are so important to Muslim religious beliefs.

Karen Armstrong, a former Roman Catholic nun who is a leading authority on Islam, explains it as follows:

> In Islam, Muslims have looked for God in history. Their sacred scripture, the Qur'an, gave them a historical mission. Their chief duty was to create a just community in which all members, even the most weak and vulnerable, were treated with absolute respect. The experience of building such a society and living in it would give them intimations of the divine, because they would be living in accordance with God's will. A Muslim had to redeem history, and that meant that state affairs were not a distraction from spirituality but the stuff of religion itself. The political well-being of the Muslim community was a matter of

supreme importance. Like any religious ideal it was almost impossibly difficult to implement in the flawed and tragic conditions of history, but after each failure Muslims had to get up and begin again.[5]

Historical mission. Absolute respect. God's will. Muslim community. Taken together, the phrases succinctly sum up the beliefs that inform traditional Muslim views on globalization.

We have already considered Islam's sense of "historical mission," a trait it shares with other paths that see themselves as *the* universal truth. What is meant by "God's will" should also be clear. That leaves "absolute respect" and the "Muslim community." Both must be understood in the broadest sense and cannot be decoupled.

To show absolute respect you must treat someone with absolute justice. That holds for both individuals and the community. On both accounts, Muslim popular opinion holds that globalization falls far short. The prevailing feeling is that the process of globalization is exploitative of individuals and destructive of Islamic culture. It is thus disrespectful of both, and profoundly unjust.

> Historical mission. God's will. Absolute respect. Muslim community. Taken together, the phrases succinctly sum up the beliefs that inform traditional Muslim views on globalization. But to show absolute respect you must treat someone with absolute justice—both individuals and the community—and the prevailing feeling is that the process of globalization is exploitative of individuals and destructive of Islamic culture.

Justice is a cornerstone of Islamic belief and, ideally, of praxis. It extends to every aspect of life because Islam holds that all of creation belongs to Allah alone. No distinction is made between the secular and sacred. There is no rendering unto Caesar. Everything is sacred, and God, acting through the Qur'an and Muslim law and tradition, dictates how a Muslim is to conduct himself at all times, regardless of the activity. It follows that if you are a Muslim, and you perceive injustice, as with globalization, then it is your duty to oppose the cause of the injustice for the well-being of the Muslim community.

Here's Armstrong again:

> Social justice [is] the crucial virtue of Islam. Muslims were commanded as their first duty to build a community (*ummah*) characterized by practical compassion, in which there was a fair distribution of wealth. This was far more important than any doctrinal teaching about God. In fact the Qur'an has a negative view of theological speculation, which it calls *zannah*, self-indulgent whimsy about ineffable matters that nobody can ascertain one way or the other. It seemed pointless to argue about such abstruse dogmas; far more crucial was the effort (*jihad*) to live in the way God had intended for human beings. The political and social welfare of the ummah would have sacramental value for Muslims.[6]

Muhammad was a merchant, and Islam is certainly not anti-entrepreneurial. However, the faith sets strict guidelines for economic activities. For example, usury (*riba*) is not permitted as a safeguard against exploiting those in financial need. While Muslim nations have long bowed to the dictates of international banking and thus charge and offer interest (sometimes calling it "commission" or "partnership"), the Qur'anic dictate retains its theoretical importance as a guiding principle of Islamic economics. Combined with *zakat,* the Islamic requirement to contribute a portion of one's wealth toward the aid of the poor and the community, it underscores the importance of striving for economic justice through fair and charitable behavior.

"Every individual has to give or spend beyond his/her direct needs, on the needy individuals and for the social well-being. In this way, Islam guards the socio-economic justice and solidarity conceptually and practically, while it considers the individual and his/her activities the basis for the human and material development," says Fathi Osman, an Egyptian-born scholar of Islam.[7]

Globalization, with its emphasis on laissez-faire capitalism, is in conflict with Islam's basic economic philosophy. However, as we have seen, it is not just the international market system's negative impact on individuals that concerned Muslims find upsetting. Globalism's collective impact on the Muslim world is of equal concern because of its perceived undermining of Islamic society and the economic systems of Muslim nations. For many Muslims, globalization is little more than neocolonialism, with the United States seen as its leading proponent, Israel (which many Muslims view as an extension of U.S. Middle East oil policy) as globalization's stalking dog, and the

Muslim world's political and economic elite its willing coconspirator. Among those who feel this way, the anger is palpable. In their view, globalization is nothing less than a direct assault on Islam. A 1998 issue of the *American Journal of Islamic Sciences,* published by a Virginia-based organization whose editorial and advisory boards boast some of the most esteemed scholars of Islam living in the United States, makes clear the depth of this view, which has only become more pronounced following September 11, 2001.

"It is no accident that most international hot spots are located in the Muslim world," wrote Ibrahim M. Abu-Rabi', codirector of the Macdonald Center for the Study of Islam and Christian-Muslim Relations at Hartford Seminary. "The main reason for this is the West's refusal to come to terms with a system of values other than its own.... A major dilemma facing the contemporary Muslim world is safeguarding universal cultural diversity and pluralism in the face of mounting American hegemony." The United States, Rabi' maintains, "has begun to mount a war against its new universal enemies...the 'menace' of Islam or Islamic 'terrorism' or 'fundamentalism.' The entire Islamic world, with its cultural and ethnic complexity, has been reduced and atomized into these terms."[8]

Also commenting in the journal, M. A. Muqtedar Khan, a political science professor at Adrian College in Michigan, warned:

> If the West, Israel, secular Muslim elites, and global capital are allowed to reshape Muslim values and Muslim identity, the subsequent actions of Muslims will be in the interests of these actors and will do

untold harm to Muslims themselves. Thus it is important that the cultural assault of globalization be resisted. Identity must be guarded jealously, lest one is enticed inadvertently into subjugation in the name of globalization.[9]

Even secular Western Muslims often share this sense of Islamic culture under siege. Bilal El-Amine was born into a family of Shi'ite Muslim *mullahs*, or religious scholars, in south Lebanon, a region embroiled in civil war and Arab-Israeli conflict for all of his almost forty years. His immediate family was, however, "very Americanized" as a result of his father's moving his brood to Saudi Arabia for employment with the U.S. military. College followed in North Carolina, and after stints in Washington, D.C., and, briefly, in Egypt, El-Amine settled in New York, a restless city he says suits his own personality.

Today, El-Amine calls himself an atheist whose Muslim identity is "political." A founding editor of the anti-globalization, anti-capitalist journal *Left Turn*, El-Amine says his intensity of political activism was born out of a sense that the West, and particularly the United States, has treated the Muslim world "hypocritically," lending support to Israel, which he calls a "racist, imperialist nation" while punishing Muslim countries such as Iraq for not conforming to Western notions of human rights and settling disputes through negotiated compromise. The economic and military power of the United States, he says, is used to impose an unjust Pax Americana that above all serves Washington's political and corporate interests.

"Growing up in south Lebanon, I came to respect the resistance movements.... I have no affinity for religious fundamentalists," he says. "But the U.S. helped create the most radical lunatic elements among the fundamentalists through its policies. Nine-eleven was a horrific act, but I reacted differently because of growing up in Lebanon. I had seen war. It was always there in my life. To me, the best description of what happened to the World Trade Center was a case of blowback—unintended consequences of what the U.S. has done to exploit and degrade the Muslim world in order to maintain control over oil supplies."

Despite such sentiments, ordinary Muslims have by no means rejected aspects of Western globalization that serve their interests. El-Amine lives in New York, not Cairo, and speaks of socialism, his preferred economic system, as a global movement furthered by the Internet and other communications breakthroughs. "Muslims love to live in the U.S. but also love to hate it. Many openly claim that the U.S. is a terrorist state, but they continue to live in it. Their decision to live here is testimony that they would rather live here than anywhere else. As an Indian Muslim, I know for sure that nowhere on earth, including India, will I get the same sense of dignity and respect that I have received in the U.S.," Khan, the Adrian College professor, wrote soon after the al-Qaeda attacks on the World Trade Center and Pentagon.[10]

Even those whose actions would seem to earn them a place at the head of the rejectionist camp embrace aspects of the process that advance their cause. Sheikh Omar Abdel Rahman, the blind Egyptian cleric whose followers tried to bring down the World Trade Center with a 1993 truck bombing, continued his war against Cairo's secular Muslim government from Brooklyn, New York. Osama bin Laden employed global communications and international financial manipulations to execute terrorist plots halfway around the world from where he sat in the Afghan mountains strategizing about the same Trade Center twin towers. Call it the globalization of terror.

Abdel Rahman and bin Laden are by no means the Muslim norm, however. Whatever their misgivings about Western culture, millions of Muslims from Asia and Africa have moved to Europe and America not to cause trouble but to seek the economic advantages, political freedoms, and personal choices unavailable in their homelands. In the United States, France, and Great Britain—to give just three examples—Islam has become or is near becoming the second largest faith group after Christianity. Meanwhile, Muslim nations now follow the Western Gregorian calendar, and American-style shopping malls complete with Planet Hollywood and McDonald's (minus the pork sausages) can be found in Saudi Arabia, enticing more to embrace Western living. The impact has changed the Muslim and non-Muslim worlds alike. Globalization is never a one-way flow, even if the exchange is tilted, for now at least, in favor of America and the West.

"Paradoxically, the cultural Westernization of the Muslim world is one of the causes behind the demographic Islamization of the West," says Ali A. Mazrui, director of the Institute of Global Cultural Studies at the State University of New York at Binghamton. "The cultural Westernization of the Muslims contributed to the 'brain drain' that lured Muslim professionals and experts from their native lands to jobs and educational institutions in North America and the European Union."

Mazrui goes on to wonder if, as education in many Muslim nations has to varying degrees been Westernized, "it is now the turn of education in the West to become partially Islamicized?" Should that occur in tandem with other advances by Islamic thought in the West, Mazrui says that Islam—at the moment "a net loser from both homogenization and hegemonization"—could one day become globalization's net winner.[11]

Some Muslims fear that embracing globalization means an inevitable decline in Islamic values. However, there are Muslim communities living primarily in the developing world that adhere closely to their group identities while embracing what they see as globalization's positive aspects. Two such groups are the estimated fifteen-million-strong Nizari Isma'ilis led by the Aga Khan, and the much smaller (about one million) Daudi Bohras Isma'ilis. Both groups are part of Islam's minority Shi'ite branch, which broke from the far larger Sunni branch over conflicts involving political successors to the Prophet Muhammad. Shi'ites, dominant in Iran and El-Amine's south Lebanon, are often viewed as being among the most antagonistic toward globalization. In fact, it's a stereotype shot full of holes, even in Iran.

Thomas L. Friedman, the New York Times Pulitzer Prize–winning foreign affairs columnist, has written often about the desire of younger Iranians to taste globalization's fruits without surrendering their Muslim identities. "They are connected to the world via the Internet or satellite dishes—and they like what they see," he says. "They want the good life, a good job, more individual freedom and more connections with the outside world—and they are increasingly angry that they don't have those things. They embrace Islam, but they don't want it to occupy every corner of their lives."[12]

Both the Nizari and Daudi Bohras Isma'ilis (and Iranian Shi'ites to a lesser degree) adhere to a spiritual doctrine unknown among Sunni Muslims, who constitute roughly 85 percent of Muslims. In the Sunni world, political authorities hold sway, generally in alliance with the religious leaders. In the Shi'ite world, primary allegiance is to religious authority. The Nizari and Daudi Bohras sects, whose members live across national boundaries, place mystic power in their leaders, who historically have been the source of all spiritual and temporal authority (the latter now much limited by the modern world).

The Nizari are led by the Aga Khan, a dapper, liberal, Harvard-educated man who runs his religious empire from outside Paris. He is one of the world's wealthiest men (his playboy father was married for a while to the Hollywood star Rita Hayworth). His community spreads across twenty-five nations, with large concentrations in India, East Africa, and to a lesser degree in Western Europe and North America. The Aga Khan's business interests are also global, as are his charitable cultural, educational, and economic development projects; the Aga Khan Foundation, headquartered in Switzerland, is the world's second largest philanthropic foundation engaged in development work. The Nizari are generally highly Westernized in dress and outlook, and the

The Nizari Isma'ilis, a group of about fifteen million Shi'ite Muslims under the spiritual leadership of the Aga Khan, generally embrace globalization's positive aspects. A well-known philanthropist who sees Qur'anic principles as his mandate, the Aga Khan regularly lectures before international forums on the need to respect cultural diversity, engage in charitable efforts, and respect human dignity in a globalized world. Aga Khan, who traces his lineage to the Prophet Muhammad's cousin and son-in-law Ali ibn Abi Talaib, regularly lectures before international forums on the need to respect cultural diversity, engage in charitable efforts, and respect human dignity in a globalized world.

Islam and religion in general, he makes clear, are the basis for his concerns and actions. "Philanthropy and charitable giving hold a very central place in the teachings of the Holy Qur'an, the writing of Islamic thinkers, and the history of Muslims in all parts and cultures of the Islamic world," the Aga Khan told a gathering in Pakistan in 2000. "Islam's clear and explicit injunction is to share resources beyond one's reasonable commitments, and to care for those in need."[13]

The Daudi Bohras present even more of a challenge to the image of Islam as inherently hostile to globalization. Led by a religious leader known as the *da'i al-mutlaq* (currently filled by Muhammad Burhanuddin) who asserts strict control over his followers, the Daudi Bohras freely mix orthodox Isma'ili dress and practice with wholehearted acceptance of Western education, modern communications technology, and global travel. "We must learn and derive benefits from Western societies without becoming enslaved by them," Syedna Burhanuddin has said (Syedna is an honorific title normally attached to his name). "While we focus on worldly and material success we must at all times remain aware of our religious obligations. *Deen* ("religion") and *duniya* ("the secular world") must coexist within us in harmony."[14]

The majority of Daudi Bohras, descendents of a Hindu ethnic group who converted to Islam about one thousand years ago, are based around Mumbai (formerly Bombay) in western India, but sect members also live in some fifty other nations. Outwardly, they generally appear highly conservative. In the words of South Asia scholar Jonah Blank, "the Bohras uphold most aspects of Islamic orthopraxy as faithfully as any Taliban priest could wish." They avoid paying or charging interest on loans. They all tend to dress in the same prescribed, modest manner. "At the same time, they eagerly adopt any and every aspect of modern or Western culture that is not specifically forbidden."

Sound contradictory? Blank doesn't think so.

> Most aspects of "modern" society that the Bohras reject are not really modern at all. The Bohra clergy urges the faithful to renounce alcohol, drugs, and sexual promiscuity. But are these really the hallmarks of modern society? People all over the world have been brewing liquor, ingesting all manner of narcotics, and engaging in every conceivable sexual practice since the dawn of recorded history. Rejection of these practices is anti-modern only if modern society is defined solely by its vices.[15]

The Nizari and Daudi Bohras Isma'ili represent a very small slice of Islamic society today. Moreover, the groups' openness to what they deem positive about globalization is as much a function of their desire to maintain the cohesiveness of far-flung minority communities as it is a continuation of historical Isma'ili openness to science, mysticism, and a wide variety of ideas in general. Still, they underscore what Hatem Bazian and Sayyid M. Syeed, both Sunni Muslims living in the United States, have also emphasized.

"We Muslims who live in America have a unique view of this globalization," Syeed says. "The desire in the Muslim world to interact with America is tremendous, whether they like America or not. If we share the best values that America has to offer—pluralism, democracy, racial diversity, respect for human rights, women's rights—I feel the Muslim world will respond positively. We need to transmit the American success story to the world."

Syeed admits that his view of globalization is tempered by his being an American. Within the Muslim world at large, he also acknowledges, his views remain in the minority. "There is a millennium of suspicion and distortion in the Muslim world toward the West. Now that America leads the West, the suspicion and distortion is directed against U.S. government policies, but not America as such," he says.

In many respects, the future of Islam will determine the future of the world, and with it the course of globalization. If the rejectionists dominate Islam, conflict will intensify because the forces of globalization, as an extension of Western values, will no more back down than will Islam's more militant proponents. But if modernists such as Syeed, Bazian, and the Aga Khan get their message across, globalization in the Islamic world just might come to mean more than Jennifer Lopez. Nothing personal, J.Lo, but that would serve us all.

3

Hinduism:
CREATING GLOBAL KARMA

IT'S WEDNESDAY EVENING at an apartment complex along the high-tech business corridor that juts northwest out of Washington, D.C. Much of the complex is given over to temporary corporate housing, but not the second floor apartment of Yash and Pallavi Malhotra. They've lived six years in Gaithersburg, Maryland, a testament to their suspension between the land of their birth and the land of their livelihood. But it's Wednesday evening and time for *satsang,* a couple of hours of prayer, reflection, and chanting to the accompaniment of a traditional *mridunga* drum, with like-minded others gathered in the spare bedroom they've turned into a miniature temple. Garland-draped statues and paintings of various Hindu deities cover an altar and beckon believers to *puja,* or devotional worship. Afterward, the dozen or so adults move to the living room floor to share a traditional Indian meal of *sag paneer, dhal,* and rice that was first consecrated to Lord Krishna, one of

Hinduism's most widely worshipped deities. The same Lord Krishna smiled in an animated video playing silently on a television screen positioned behind one side of the circle of diners.

Indian high-tech workers have flocked to communities across America that mirror Gaithersburg, lured like the Malhotras by well-paying jobs and a chance to experience the new global culture. In the case of Yash and his wife, Pallavi, however, the payoff turned out to be more than just economic advancement and a bit of adventure. Halfway around the world from their native India, the Malhotras, to their surprise, found themselves embracing their spiritual roots. That they did so in a branch of Hinduism brought to America by an Indian guru who introduced it to the disaffected sons and daughters of the 1960s, and who in turn reintroduced the Malhotras to the religion of their birth, is another of globalization's quirky footnotes.

"In India I went to a temple once in a blue moon. But what is the goal of life and what is God?—that was not clear to me," says Yash, who works for a computer software company. "When we came to the U.S. we started visiting temples looking for connections to what was familiar. Suddenly temples and questions about life became important to me. Then we visited the Potomac [Maryland] temple, met the devotees, and found we were comfortable. Soon I became interested in the philosophy, and I found something. I found happiness."

Plunked down in a foreign environment, the Malhotras' native culture gained new meaning for them. What had been life's wallpaper became, in its absence, the couple's anchor. What did it mean to be Hindu? How do the values of Washington's middle class suburbs mesh, or conflict, with those of the *Vedic* tradition, Hinduism's ancient scriptural bedrock? And what did it mean to ponder these questions using materials largely written for and by Westerners but drawn from *sanatana dharma*, Sanskrit for the "eternal tradition," that Hindus believe is the essence of their, and all, religion?

The Malhotras are by no means the only ethnic Indians who, away from their homeland, have been drawn to the International Society for Krishna Consciousness (ISKCON), commonly known as the Hare Krishnas. About half of the estimated eighty thousand congregants at the movement's fifty temples in North America are ethnic Indian Hindus, say ISKCON officials. Established in New York in the mid-1960s by Swami Bhaktivedanta Prabhupada, who was then nearly seventy years old, ISKCON is based on Vaishnava Hinduism, a practice focused on devotional worship of the incarnations of the god Vishnu, and in particular the popular deity Krishna.

The success of ISKCON in attracting ethnic Hindus is not surprising, since more than half of the world's nearly one billion Hindus ascribe to Vaishnavite practices.[1] That success allowed ISKCON to survive the "cult" status and internal problems that decimated its membership after the sixties' zeitgeist in which it was planted faded away. Additionally, ISKCON's ethnic Indian component says much about globalization's impact on Hinduism, as well as the complex set of Hindu theological attitudes relating to the process by which economic and cultural globalization are changing the world. Those attitudes are as varied as India, a vast subcontinent of a nation that is home to nearly a thousand local languages, a nation that is at once largely rural yet also boasting the city of Bangalore, a leading center of the global communications revolution—and a place where high-tech workers perform puja to their computers.[2]

"It's hard to imagine the Internet as we know it without [the contributions of] India and Indian technologists," says Daniel Yergin, a leading commentator on globalization.[3]

One approaches Hinduism much like the blind man approaches an elephant; the subject is so vast that conclusions can vary widely depending upon the part touched first. Of all the major faiths, Hinduism is the toughest to categorize, the most elastic in its authority, the most diverse in its range of accepted beliefs and practices. Hinduism is a cultural amalgam as much as it is a religious tradition, more a collection of traditions than a unified tradition, deeply conservative at its core yet libertarian, and liberal, at its edges. In short, Hinduism is to religion what cats are to a herder. Perhaps the most general statement one may make about Hindu thought is that it fully acknowledges the principle that people are different in infinite ways, which is why there exists an infinite number of paths to the one supreme truth, the unified godhead known as Brahman. Hence, Hinduism's unlimited number of deities, which reflect the universe's uncountable forms and functions. It should come as no surprise, then, that many of the details of globalization are highly problematic from a Hindu standpoint, but that there is also much within Hinduism to support the process itself.

Just as the Western perception that Hinduism is polytheistic is a simplistic understanding of its deeper monism, so is Hinduism's reputation for being an otherworldly, antimaterialistic path a misstating of its deeper comprehension of the human need for material security and achievement. Consider the four basic human needs, or goals, recognized by Vedic Hinduism. They are *dharma, artha, kama,* and *moksha.* Dharma refers to the need to live in harmony with one's personal nature, society, and eternal wisdom or face unending trouble. Kama refers to the human need for pleasure, sexual and otherwise. It goes hand in hand with artha, the accumulation of wealth. Artha is the Hindu recognition of the human impulse to engage in economic activity and nation building. "[Hinduism] grants, not only that success is a requisite for supporting a household and discharging one's civic responsibilities, but that its achievements confer dignity and self-respect," notes religion scholar Huston Smith.[4]

The fourth need is moksha, spiritual liberation, for which the first three are mere preparation. Hindu sages have taught for more than four thousand years that moksha trumps all other

> Hindu thought fully acknowledges the principle that people are different in infinite ways, which is why there exists an infinite number of paths to the one supreme truth, which is the unified godhead known as Brahman. Hinduism's unlimited number of deities reflects the universe's uncountable forms and functions. It should come as no surprise, then, that many of the details of globalization are highly problematic from a Hindu standpoint, but that there is also much within Hinduism to support the process itself.

human needs. Moksha means release from the karmic cycle of birth and rebirth, and is the culmination of the human experience. It is also why ultimately the pleasures and acquisitions of material life are never fully satisfying.

But Hinduism views human life through a very long lens. Spiritual evolution occurs over many lifetimes; just how many depends upon individual progress. It is a progression, however, and the first three needs must be fulfilled before the *atman,* the eternal soul within us all, is moved to seek liberation. Here's Smith again:

> Pleasure, success and duty are not what we really want, the Hindus say; what we really want is to be, to know, and to be happy. No one wants to die, to be in the dark about things, or to be miserable. Pleasure, success and duty are only approximations of what we really want; they are apertures through which our true wants come through to us [which are] liberation from everything that distances us from infinite being, infinite awareness, and infinite bliss.[5]

The goal of life is liberation of the soul. Until then, how is one to live, and how does it relate to globalization?

As stated, Hinduism recognizes the value of material wealth. But the path also makes clear that "commercial goals are secondary to the goal of life. To the degree that globalization emphasizes consumerism and the creating and satisfying of desires, it is out of alignment with Hindu beliefs, which are about taming desires," says David Frawley, a convert to Hinduism who runs the American

Institute of Vedic Studies in Santa Fe, New Mexico, and who also goes by the name Vamadeva Shastri.

The Laws of Manu is an ancient Hindu text (scholars say it could be as much as four thousand years old) of "injunctions, prohibitions and moral pronouncements concerning every important aspect of social and religious life in ancient India."[6] It says this of desire: "Desire is never extinguished by the enjoyment of desired objects; it only grows stronger like a fire [fed] with clarified butter" (2:94).

Swami Agnivesh, a former Indian state legislator, educator, and prominent environmental and social activist, states the same in more stark language. To Agnivesh, the untamed desire to consume equates with "organized greed," which he considers a hallmark of economic globalization: "In the global economy, the monster of greed threatens to enjoy a longer leash and farther reach." Multinational corporations, he laments, "are able to manipulate the market forces and influence domestic economic and industrial policies to maximize their profits. In that sense, globalization has unleashed the dogs of greed in the poorer societies of the world."[7]

Living means participating in life. We make decisions and take actions—all of which create karma. This basic Hindu doctrine means that everything we do has an effect, no matter how subtle. One act sets in motion the next. Every act has ethical consequences—which is to say they are bound to have repercussions for us and for others. Hindus believe that karma also determines our future rebirths, that how you handle this life determines how you begin the next one. Handling this one in accordance with sanatana dharma gives you a leg up on the next. Live "out of alignment" and you create karma that impedes the evolutionary process of liberation. It's not very different from the biblical advice, "As you sow, so shall you reap." It works that way for individuals, and it works that way for society. Says Agnivesh:

> While the love for material possession drives the culture of greed, the caring culture is driven by the love for our fellow human beings. It is the nature of love to care and to share, and share, if need be, sacrificially.... We cannot maintain a wasteful and indulgent lifestyle and remain caring in our outlook. The practical truth is that nobody has enough resources with which to care for anybody else, after all his many and ever-multiplying cravings are satisfied. The sea has limits, says an ancient aphorism, but human desire has none.[8]

Consumption driven by desire rather than need hurts the individual. It also hurts the environment and nonhuman life, the latter viewed as souls on a lower rung of the liberation ladder. "Hinduism rejects the 'homosapien centered' worldview," notes Agnivesh.[9] The entire world is one divine society.

For traditional Hindus, both the earth and nonhuman life are sacred, and concerns that transnational corporations, abetted by compliant or corrupt governments, have turned both into commodities are cause for additional opposition to globalization. I say *traditional* Hindus because, as many Hindus will tell you, Hindu societies that the traditionalists see as spiritually compromised have fared no better than others in protecting the environment. Vasudha Narayanan, a professor of religion at the University of Florida, blames this on globalization's corrosive influence. "The seductive power of consumer goods and the easy profits promised by large industries that have scant respect for the environment were powerful enough to overcome any vestiges of respect for theology," she says.[10]

Bhumi mata is Hinduism's Sanskrit term referring to the religion's belief that the earth is more than an inanimate object. Rather, Vedic belief holds that the earth is the Divine Mother associated with the goddess Prthivi, who along with the god Dyaus Pita, Father Sky, are the parents of all the gods. As such, the earth is an extension of the God consciousness that pervades the entire universe and is to be treated with respect, even worshipped, and certainly not abused. "That Hindus have forgotten their connection with the earth is perhaps their greatest falling from their older and deeper traditions," says Frawley.

Hinduism is traditionally associated with vegetarianism, but the truth is that many Hindus do eat meat, and Vedic literature is replete with references to animal sacrifices (including cows, despite the veneration

Hindus who argue against globalization invoke the principal of *ahimsa*, or nonviolence toward all life. The earth is seen as an extension of the God consciousness that pervades the entire universe and is to be treated with respect. Globalization's undermining of traditional Hindu social systems is also seen as a form of violence toward Hindu culture and religion.

they also receive as symbols of divine benevolence). Like so much about Hinduism, however, contradictory references also abound concerning meat eating. In this case they expound the benefits of not eating meat to avoid creating bad karma by inflicting harm on another living entity and interrupting the progression of its soul toward human birth and eventual liberation. "Meat can never be obtained without injury to living creatures, and injury to sentient beings is detrimental to [the attainment of] heavenly bliss; let him therefore shun [the use of] meat," say the Laws of Manu (5:48).

According to some sources, the status of cows was elevated to the level they enjoy today over the previous millennia in part as a reaction to the Islamic invasion of India. Muslims ate cows, so protecting them became a symbol of Hindu resistance that was incorporated into the principal of *ahimsa,* or nonviolence toward all life. Ahimsa is another often-cited reason given by Hindu critics of globalization, who maintain the process is causing great harm to the world's poor and the environment.

I have so far focused on Hindu opposition to globalization based generally on concerns for individual spiritual advancement. There is, however, another set of reasons used by Hindus in arguing against globalization. Ahimsa straddles the two sets of arguments. The second set may be categorized as cultural concerns, and they are little different than those voiced by other non-Western traditions that also see globalization as a Trojan horse. Hindu activists also decry globalization as just a latter-day form of economic and cultural hegemony undermining traditional Hindu systems. Once again, the United States, as the world's leading economic and cultural power, is viewed as the main villain.

"The American view of globalization is people all over the world becoming American or adapting an American consumerist lifestyle," says Frawley, a leading American scholar and advocate of Hinduism. "We must recognize that this is not true globalization at all and reflects a narrow point of view, not planetary thinking." He goes on:

> The negative side of globalization is a disturbing neo-colonialism—the continued projection of Western and European civilization and its values for everyone, just as in the colonial era. The new multinational corporations appear like a continuation of old colonial businesses like the East India Company.... The West considers its culture to be universal, though it is only one of many in the world.... The old colonial rulers had the same view of their culture as the best for everyone on the planet. The West sees not only its scientific view of the world as good for all, but also its intellectual culture and its religions as the best, if not the only legitimate ones. While Americans are proud of Asians wearing blue jeans they are quite suspicious of Americans wearing turbans or chanting Sanskrit *mantras*.

Mohandas Karamchand Gandhi, better known as Mahatma Gandhi (*Mahatma* is an honorific meaning "great soul"), was the father of India's nonviolent campaign for political independence from British rule. He was also an early product of globalization; he was educated in Britain and made his reputation in South Africa working on behalf of that nation's Indian community prior to returning to his homeland and entering the independence struggle. Gandhi was no fan of globalization; in his day there was nothing "neo" about its connection to colonialism. He preferred localization, which he articulated through the concept of *swadeshi,* which means local, Indian-controlled commerce and industry. Gandhi was often photographed working a spinning wheel turning out cotton yarn. It was an expression of swadeshi. His point was to show that India could meet its own needs for yarn without resorting to importing it from Britain, which was more expensive, fostered dependency, and undermined village economies. Gandhi said almost a century ago:

> Because of its neglect of swadeshi, the nation has been ruined. Three crores [an Indian term for ten million] in India, that is, a tenth of the total population of the country, get only one meal a day, just plain bread and no more. Crores of rupees are annually lost to foreign countries. If this wealth of crores could remain in the country, we would be able to save our starving countrymen. Thus, our economic well-being is also bound up with swadeshi, and in its observance there lies compassion for living beings.[11]

Although generally considered in economic terms, Gandhi maintained that the swadeshi spirit—using local resources—also acted to safeguard Hinduism because it anchored Hindus to their ancestral faith and home. Today, Hindu nationalists argue that swadeshi is an indigenous Indian alternative to foreign-dominated globalization. One such person is C. Abraham Varghese, a Mumbai (formerly Bombay) management consultant and a fervent Hindu activist. Advocating swadeshi, he maintains, does not make you a Luddite. It's simply the South Asian version of "Buy American."

"The concept of swadeshi is not the exclusion of all technologies," says Varghese, whose pen name is Vasuki, the name of a Hindu snake deity. "There is no commercial or technical or managerial activity engaged [in] by any foreign company in India which cannot be done by an Indian equally efficiently and at much lower costs.... Swadeshi is a conviction that no foreign country should profit from an activity which we can do for ourselves in a cheaper and equally efficient manner as any other country."[12]

Swadeshi is one aspect of the Hindu counterreaction to globalization. Another is the rise of political groups often labeled Hindu "fundamentalist," which some Hindus argue is a misnomer given how diffuse Hinduism truly is. Combining militant nationalism with religion, groups such as the Bharatiya Janata Parishad, Viswa Hindu Parishad, Shiv Sena, and Rashtriya Swayamsevek Sangh (a former member of which assassinated Gandhi for being too sympathetic toward Muslims) have sought to assert Hindu supremacy over India's body politic. In the process, they have clashed with Indian Muslims and Christians, whom they accuse of seeking to convert Hindus and harming India's dominant Hindu culture.

Hindu texts divide time into four periods called *yugas*, during which the universe is said to form and dissolve over and over, and unendingly. The yugas correspond to the mythical life span of Brahman, the godhead, and the last of the four yugas is *kali yuga*, "the age of strife." During kali yuga virtue is said to diminish and chaos descends upon a world hurtling toward destruction. We are, according to Hindu tradition, about five thousand years into the current kali yuga, and have more than four million more to go before the world is destroyed and the cycle of birth and death begins anew. To borrow from Huston Smith, "exhaled and then inhaled, the world is God's respiration."[13] Mention the problems of globalization in the context of kali yuga and a knowing Hindu is likely to give you a look that says, "What else did you expect?"

Yet it has not been all bad for sanatana dharma, the eternal tradition. Globalization has disrupted traditional Hindu ways, and much of globalization's values are in conflict with those of Hinduism. But it has also helped spread the teachings. Hinduism has been globalized along with American fast food. The spread of Hinduism is in some ways obvious—the ISKCON satsang in Maryland is one example. In other ways, say some Hindus, the spread has been subtle. Let's enumerate the obvious first.

Despite historic religious restrictions against members of high castes traveling outside India, Hindus have done so for centuries, although not always happily. In the nineteenth century, the global Hindu diaspora was created when large numbers of Indians were shipped "under conditions of savage exploitation," as University of California at Los Angeles

> Diaspora Hindus stay connected to each other, and to the religion, through various global movements:
> - social action programs such as those led by Pandurang Shastri Athavale, who stresses *shramabhakti* ("devotional labor")
> - charismatic gurus, or master teachers, such as Sathya Sai Baba, who teaches a more traditional form of Hindu devotion
> - the International Society for Krishna Consciousness, commonly known as the Hare Krishnas, whose temples in the West are home to ethnic Hindu and Western converts alike

history professor Vinay Lal notes, to Fiji, Mauritius, Trinidad, Malaysia, Guyana, Surinam, South Africa, and elsewhere to be indentured workers on sugar, tea, and rubber plantations.[14] Today, diaspora Hindus stay connected to each other, and to the religion, through global movements as varied as those led by Pandurang Shastri Athavale, who stresses *shramabhakti* ("devotional labor") on behalf of social action programs, and Sathya Sai Baba, who is said to create "sacred" ash and other substances out of thin air, and who teaches a more traditional form of Hindu devotion centered on the guru, a master teacher believed capable of advancing the spiritual development of others.

Lal notes that diaspora Hindus often embrace Hindu nationalism and "routinely invoke Indian civilization with a self-assurance that in India would be both mocked and contested."[15] They are, at times, more Hindu than the Indian Hindus, who, as was the case for Yash Malhotra, may consider Hinduism no more deeply than they do the songbird's ambient sound. Lal might have been talking about Sudeep Roy, a University of California at Berkeley undergraduate and a second-generation follower of Sathya Sai Baba. Roy was born in India but has lived most of his life in the San Francisco Bay Area. Retaining his "Indian-ness" is important, he says, which for him equates with Hinduism. "We're Americans but at the same time we're Hindus," he says of his parents and California Indian friends. "For many of us, Hindu identity is Indian identity."

His cousins in India go out on dates, but Roy, who is president of his school's Hindu Student Council, says he is inclined toward having his parents find him a bride in the traditional Indian Hindu manner. His Indian relatives are meat eaters, but Roy's family is vegetarian. "It's odd, isn't it? I'm more traditional in California than they are in India. Globalization has turned things topsy-turvy."

In 1893 Swami Vivekananda created a stir at the first Parliament of the World's Religions in Chicago and is cred-ited with laying the foundation for the many Hindu teach-ers who later came West and developed large followings by presenting Hinduism as possessing universal truths and spiritual growth techniques that are ideally suited for a plu-ralistic age. Among them have been Paramahansa Yogananda, Maharishi Mahesh Yogi, Swami Vishnu Devananda, Krishnamurti, Swami Muktananda, and Swami Satchidananda. Then there have been the myriad Westerners they influenced—from the Beatles to one-time Harvard professor and psychedelic visionary Baba Ram Das—who also helped make hatha yoga postures a staple of Western exercise classes and mantra meditation a staple of stress reduction and other self-help programs. The global-ization of Hinduism, its acceptance as a valid spiritual path *in* the West and *for* Westerners, has in many ways been nothing short of spectacular, particularly in view of its vast differences from traditional Judeo-Christian beliefs.

Bhakti Tirtha Swami Krishnapada is a prime example of Hinduism taking root among nonethnic Hindus. Born into an African American Baptist family as John E. Favors, he was a child evangelist in the Cleveland area before study-ing psychology and Eastern philosophies at Princeton University. He also worked with the Reverend Martin Luther King, Jr., who, Krishnapada is quick to note, often acknowledged the influence that Gandhi's writings on non-violence had on his own strategies in the civil rights move-ment. Then, in the early 1970s, Favors joined ISKCON and became Krishnapada. Today, he travels the world for the organization, spending much of his time in Africa.

Globalization, he says, is designed above all to further Western interests "because that's where the multinationals' leaders live." Globalization has also diminished aspects of India's Hindu culture. Yet the revolution in global commu-nications has also helped spread Hindu teachings and keeps Hindus in touch with each other, he says. Moreover, look beyond globalization's immediate impact and a deep-er dynamic may be seen at work, one that mirrors a subtler globalization of Hindu teachings, he says.

Global marketing has become so competitive that transnational companies have to refine their strategies for reaching potential markets, he explains. That means com-panies are striving harder to understand customer needs. It may be for a manipulative purpose—to sell whatever—but it also means "getting to know more about the whole person. We see this as something healthy because it takes into effect the deeper aspects of a person.... People want to feel valued and appreciated.... From a Vedic perspective, anything that helps people interact better ultimately helps them in their pursuit of the godhead."

Gandhi first connected to Hindu spirituality while he was a student in London. Lalit Agarwal, raised by a religious family in Assam in Eastern India, came to the United States in 1991 to study computer sciences and promptly began "exploring the waters of atheism." In 1996, he returned to the fold after meeting ISKCON devotees. He is now a software consultant and lives in Vienna, Virginia, an hour or so south of the Malhotras' Gaithersburg apartment. On Wednesday evenings he and his wife, Vanita, make the drive to be part of the satsang. "Globalization made it possible for me to see the true glory of Vedic culture," he says. "Because a tree standing with other trees is hard to discern. But here, in America, the Vedic tree stands alone and is easily discerned."

There's not much chance that the Washington suburbs will ever equal Varanasi (Banaras) as a sacred city for Hindus. The Potomac will never replace the Ganges. Yet in a globalized world, sanatana dharma can pop up anywhere. It is eternal, after all. And there's plenty of room for accommodation within Hinduism's world of multiplicity. Just ask the Malhotras and the Agarwals.

4

Judaism:
SPEAKING TRUTH TO POWER

DEUTERONOMY IS THE LAST OF THE FIVE BOOKS OF MOSES—the core of the Hebrew Bible, or Torah—that together tell a story of extraordinary breadth, from the Creation and the Garden of Eden to the death of Moses as the ancient Israelites prepare to enter the Promised Land. Deuteronomy, as befits a final volume, is a summation of sorts; it is Judaism's biblical blueprint for righteous living and includes the well-known Ten Commandments as well as the little known and long-abandoned rules for conducting ancient Temple sacrifices. For Rabbi Michael Feinberg, Deuteronomy also contains the Bible's most meaningful passages, ones that explain much about his life's work and his attitude toward globalization. The passages read:

> You shall not exploit a poor or an indigent employee, from your brothers or from your aliens who are in your land, in your gates. You shall give his pay in his day, and the sun shall not set on it—because he

is poor, and he maintains his life by it—so he won't call against you to YHWH,[1] and it will be a sin in you (Deuteronomy 24:14–15).

Feinberg, a lean, intensely passionate man, runs a coalition of religious and labor leaders who struggle to improve wages and job conditions for New York's lowest-paid workers, the often undocumented foreign-born men and women who spend long hours washing restaurant dishes, cleaning hotels and offices, toiling in sweat-shop factories, or lugging materials at construction sites. This is the aspect of globalization—the movement of unskilled laborers across national borders—that Feinberg confronts daily. It leaves him seething at what he regards as the callous disregard of transnational corporate giants and pliant governments that conspire to enrich themselves at the expense of the world's masses. "New York is a global city that for some is a nonstop party, and for others means scrounging on garbage heaps all their lives," says Feinberg. "That's the globalization I see that I oppose."

Feinberg is a rabbi in the humanistic-orientated Reconstructionist movement, Judaism's newest and smallest organized branch. Reconstructionist Judaism focuses on community life in the here and now, and Feinberg's mode of speech, the unvarnished language of labor organizers, reflects that rationalist orientation. Rabbi Arthur Waskow, in contrast, is firmly aligned with the experimental and often esoteric Jewish Renewal movement that focuses on personal spiritual development and stands outside the mainstream of Jewish religious tradition; think of it as a Jewish countercultural response to the Eastern spiritual practices that have intrigued so many Westerners in recent years. Unlike Feinberg, Waskow's speech, though equally impassioned, is rich in the language of religious metaphor. When he speaks of globalization's ills, he invokes the image of ancient Israel's bondage in Egypt and a ruler who defied God by refusing to free the Israelite slaves—Judaism's most enduring theological axis.

"Globalization is the pharaoh of our day, the absolute archetype of unaccountable power," says Waskow. "It was the enslavement of workers that brought down upon Egypt a massive ecological catastrophe [the plagues], and that's where we see globalization headed. What we need is described in Deuteronomy 17, where God puts limits on kingly power. That's relevant to globalization if you understand the passage as limiting the power of the elite few to unjustly dominate the many, which sums up the sins of globalization."

For all their outward differences, the two veteran social activists agree on this: Judaism's ethical teachings compel them to confront worldly power that is wielded unjustly—which is how they judge the actions of the captains of commerce and finance who steer the global market. And while they approach the text differently, both Feinberg and Waskow find their inspiration in the same ancient writings that have inspired Jews for thousands of years.

Judaism is the ancestral religion of the Jewish people, for whom a global existence has long been the accepted state of affairs and, in many ways, has been key to their communal survival. Globalization may be a term of recent coinage, but the multifaceted process it attempts to encompass developed slowly over many centuries, and Jews have been involved since the beginning. Geography and the hostility of other peoples left them little other choice.

When the ancient Israelites—the people to whom contemporary Jews trace their lineage—settled the Promised Land, they claimed a region at the intersection of trade and migration routes linking Europe, Asia, and Africa. Economic and cultural isolation were impossible in a land constantly traversed by merchants who imported foreign ideas and conquerors that forced Jews to adapt or perish. Over centuries, Jews were transformed from a small, inwardly focused tribal group inhabiting a sliver of eastern Mediterranean soil to a people resolute in the maintenance of their faith and culture no matter how far they relocated from their ancestral homeland. Adherence to Judaism's basic principles and practices kept them alive as a unified, if widely dispersed, people. Global Diaspora became the Jewish lot, and from it came vitality.

> Rabbi Arthur Waskow says Deuteronomy 17, in which God puts limits on kingly power, is relevant to globalization if you understand the passage as limiting the power of the elite few to unjustly dominate the many—which for him sums up the sins of globalization. The words of that chapter of the Hebrew Bible instruct the Jewish people, upon setting up their nation in the Promised Land, that the king must not be a man of another nation but one of the brethren; he must not lead the people for his own gain; he must not distract himself through excesses of women or riches; he must keep the law as given and read it every day of his life; and the king must not be proud or prejudicial in his rule.

A study by the World Jewish Congress (WJC), the leading international federation of Jewish communities and organizations, states this history forthrightly:

> The Jews are a global people. They have always supported globalization, even before the term was used and before it took on its special significance in an age of international markets and economics, cellular communications and the Internet. Jewish existence in the Diaspora has been based, for hundreds of years, on globalization, and in many periods it has been the Jews who supported and spread the concept. In reliance on their ability to build international ties connecting between different Diaspora communities, the Jews have always promoted globalization, and have served as its agents.[2]

In the Middle Ages, writes Avi Beker, the author of the WJC study, hostile civil and religious authorities restricted Jews in where they could live, in the ownership of land, and in the trades and professions open to them. But by linking with coreligionists settled in strategic commercial centers, Jews worked around the prohibitions. In doing so, they began to lay the groundwork for what became modern, transnational capitalism. Two Jewish religious traditions—*halacha* and rabbinic courts—facilitated the innovation.

Halacha, a Hebrew term, is the system of Jewish law that addresses the minutiae of interpersonal and ritual life. For tradition-minded Jews, halacha is sacrosanct and controlling of all outward behavior from day's beginning to end.

Detailed observance of halacha is today largely restricted to members of Judaism's Orthodox movement, the faith's most traditional branch but no longer its largest. In the Middle Ages, however, halacha still held powerful sway over Jews everywhere. It was the psychological and spiritual glue that bound the community by ensuring loyalty to an ethical standard, which, in turn, bred the trust that enabled Jews to engage in commerce with each other over long distances in an era before civic law could be counted upon to encourage similar trust among merchants and entrepreneurs of other faiths and nationalities. Moreover, rabbinic courts—known in Hebrew as *bet din*—stood behind the enforcement of halacha with the power to impose fines and shame Jewish offenders across territorial boundaries. Excommunication was the courts' most punitive weapon. "At a time when the Jewish community was highly cohesive and its members were mutually dependent upon one another, the possibility of excommunication represented a serious deterrent," notes the *Encyclopedia of Judaism*.[3]

Jewish success in the emerging global economy was enormous. Jews developed alternative markets when denied entry to established guilds that controlled existing commerce. Within the context of halacha they created procedures for doing business based on credit, thereby reducing the need to transport gold and other barter items over long and dangerous distances. Halacha's elasticity became evident as rabbinic scholars creatively reasoned how to allow charging interest, which previously had been frowned upon. Jews became the court bankers from Baghdad to Spain. "At the end of the seventeenth century, one quarter of the shares of the Dutch East Indies Company (the archetype of an international trading company) were held by Jews."[4]

Given their relatively small numbers, that sort of economic success was extraordinary. Still, it only amounted to a foreshadowing of what was to come, says Beker.

Contemporary Jews, he says, have managed to do even better. Above all, however, it has been American Jews, members of the most accepted Diaspora community over the millennia of Jewish history, who have outpaced all others.

> There is no doubt that in the age of globalization...
> American Jewry is reaching heights of success so
> great that they are spoken of as experiencing a
> "golden age" which surpasses in terms of scope any
> previous period in the history of Jewish life in the
> Diaspora.... The age of globalization is one in
> which the centrality of the Jewish factor becomes
> even more clear.[5]

Of course, not all Jews are wealthy. Yet for many, particularly in the United States and other Western nations, middle-class security has become the expected norm in a world still dominated by great poverty. For this, Jewish leaders take justifiable pride in their community's success. However, they also acknowledge that success has not come without great pain.

Wealth breeds jealousy, and innovation threatens entrenched power. When mixed with religious and ethnic intolerance, lethal stereotypes too often result. For Jews, that meant suffering widespread anti-Semitism, sometimes even in nations where their economic contributions were paramount to the prevailing prosperity of non-Jews. "The vast majority of multi-national corporations aren't Jewish-owned, nor do they function under halacha's ethical demands," says Rabbi Barry Freundel, an Orthodox Jew who leads a Washington, D.C., synagogue that garnered a modicum of attention in 2000 thanks to its most famous congregant, Senator Joseph Lieberman, the first Jew to run for vice president of the United States on a major party ticket. "Modern globalization isn't a Jewish thing, and it's certainly not run by Jews. Yet we get blamed."

Fear of feeding irrational anti-Semitism has kept historians, Jewish or otherwise, from fully exploring the connection between Jews and the history of economic globalization, says Beker.[6] Today, it is not uncommon for the extremist fringe of the anti-globalization movement to play on anti-Semitism in attempts to rally support. An example of this was evident in early 2002 in Moscow, where a conference of right-wing Holocaust deniers heard one speaker proclaim that "the rejection of Christianity and the cosmopolitization of humanity on the basis of the worldview of the Talmudists is the main goal of anti-Christian globalization."[7] Another prominent display of anti-Semitism was the singling out of Israel for criticism beyond that leveled at any other nation during the 2001 United Nations World Conference against Racism, Racial Discrimination, Xenophobia, and Related Intolerance of Judaism, in Durban, South Africa.

Controversy over Israel, the Jewish state, has added further fuel. Anti-globalization rallies in cities around the world have in recent years been turned into demonstrations against Israeli policies toward the Palestinians. At a massive April

2002 anti-globalization rally in Washington, D.C., for example, posters equating fascism and racism with the Star of David—a symbol of religious Judaism as well as of the nation of Israel—were in great evidence, and slogans in opposition to World Bank policies were shouted in unison with those lambasting Israel's actions.[8]

Given the benefits Jews have enjoyed from their participation in the global economy, it is little wonder they generally tend to support globalization. Combined with the hostility toward their interests they see manifested in the anti-globalization movement, it's even less surprising that few mainstream Jewish groups, including the more liberal, have taken strong public stands in conjunction with anti-globalization campaigns.

Jewish groups often do criticize globalization's darker aspects on their own, just as some Jews have been leaders in myriad movements and campaigns to end social injustices and protect natural resources. A resolution presented at the 2001 biennial convention of the Union of American Hebrew Congregations (UAHC), the synagogue umbrella agency for the liberal Reform movement in North America, notes the "degraded environment, human rights abuses and lowered labor standards, internationally and domestically" resulting from globalization. "Fundamental values of equity, democracy, and environmental protection are at stake in the way international trade is organized and governed" by the World Trade Organization and other such instruments of globalization. The document goes on to say that the UAHC is compelled to speak out on the issue because of Judaism's belief that "from the time of Creation, people from all over the world are intended to share our planet and its resources." All people are created "in the image of God," it adds, calling that an understanding of the "interconnected nature of our existence" that takes on greater importance in an era of global interaction.[9]

Despite that statement, don't expect to see Reform Jewish leaders standing shoulder to shoulder with anti-globalization activists anytime soon. "The globalization debate has sucked in a great many disparate causes, including the Arab-Israeli conflict, that give us pause," explains Mark Pelavin, associate director of the UAHC's Religious Action Center, Reform's social justice and religious freedom lobbying arm in Washington, D.C.

That is not to say that Jews are absent from the anti-globalization movement's more confrontational wing, the body of mostly young people who travel from city to city—

> The Union of American Hebrew Congregations spoke out against the "degraded environment, human rights abuses and lowered labor standards, internationally and domestically" resulting from globalization. Concerns expressed in the 2001 resolution include:
> - Fundamental values being threatened by international trade organized and governed by the World Trade Organization and other instruments of globalization
> - Judaism's belief that from the time of Creation, all people were intended to share the earth and its resources
> - The interconnected nature of our existence becomes increasingly important in this era of global interaction—because all people are created in the image of God

and sometimes, in one of globalization's ironies, easily around the globe—to stage street protests at meetings of the World Economic Forum, the International Monetary Fund, the World Bank, and other such institutions. For most of these committed activists, though, their Jewish roots do not consciously inform their efforts on behalf of the issue. An exception is Dara Silverman.

Silverman has been a Boston-based national organizer for a group called United for a Fair Economy. The group's focus is the growing income disparity between rich and poor, a condition it believes is exacerbated by globalization. She is also the founder of a locally focused Boston organization that presents "a progressive and radical Jewish voice" on economic and social issues. "A key piece is that I'm in this for the long haul," Silverman says of her work, which involves educating and training activists to confront economic issues. "For me Judaism is one of those things that sustains me."

Silverman describes herself as "pretty secular" and her connection to Judaism as more "cultural and political" than religious. Yet when asked to explain her motivation, this 1995 Bard College graduate speaks of Judaism's religious dictate to engage in *tsedakah*.

Although often translated as charity, *tsedakah* is derived from the Hebrew term for justice. Thus, within traditional Judaism the understanding is that charity is not something to be given out of pity or even altruism. Rather, it is seen as an essential part of God's plan for the just society, making tsedakah a religious obligation. Deuteronomy, again, makes this clear: "I command you, saying, You shall open your hand to your brother, to your poor, and to your indigent in your land" (Deuteronomy 15:11).

Silverman views tsedakah as a two-way street—as a process that is as important to her own spiritual development as it is to the economic enhancement of those she assists. "Your liberation is inextricably tied up in mine," she says, quoting what she said was an Australian Aboriginal expression. "It's an opportunity to work together to build community and effect change."

Anti-globalization activist Dara Silverman, who describes her connection to Judaism as "cultural and political," lives out her convictions in the following concrete ways:

- She works as an organizer for groups that seek to educate the public about growing economic disparities
- She trains activists in order to widen the circle working for economic equality
- She travels regularly to demonstrate at anti-globalization rallies

Silverman also believes that Jews—by virtue of their historic role and the economic gains they have accrued—have a special responsibility to help right globalization's inequities. Rabbi David Seidenberg, a writer and teacher who was ordained by Judaism's middle-of-the-road Conservative movement, likens that responsibility to the role that the biblical patriarch Joseph played in the development of the ancient Egyptian economic order that eventually became oppressive to Jews as well and resulted in their slavery as a people.

Joseph—he of the "coat of many colors"—was sold into bondage in Egypt by his jealous brothers, only to become an interpreter of the Pharaoh's dreams of a famine to come. That earned him the role of viceroy in charge of preparing for the predicted hard times. Joseph, Hebrew scripture tells us, proved as adept with economics as he was with dreams, and Pharaoh prospered under his guidance. But instead of showing generosity, Pharaoh, under Joseph's financial direction, used his food stocks to solidify his power over Egypt's hungry people. "And Joseph collected all the silver that was found in the land of Egypt and the land of Canaan for the grain that they were buying, and Joseph brought the silver to Pharaoh's house" (Genesis: 47:14).

"It was Joseph," says Seidenberg, "who administered this system of economic takeover. When a new Pharaoh arose, the Israelites came under the same system of control and dominance. So the power which was sweet when it protected our people's wealth became bitter when it was used to destroy our freedom."[10]

To critics of globalization such as Seidenberg, the Joseph story metaphorically sums up the Jewish responsibility toward correcting globalization's corporate ravages and the danger that Jews will face along with the world at large if the process is allowed to proceed unchecked. "Jews have a great stake in capitalism as an ideology," Seidenberg says. "It bought us great freedom from persecution, but it has also led us to develop some blind spots about its implementation which cannot be ignored."

Rabbi Michael Lerner, editor of the progressive Jewish magazine *Tikkun*, would agree that Jews, by virtue of their place "at the top of the food chain," have a special responsibility to counter globalization's negative aspects. But he would start by declaring globalization's worst aspect to be the philosophy he considers to be at the core of the process—economic gain as life's highest purpose and priority. For Lerner, one of the more visible spokespersons of liberal Judaism on the American scene, the Jewish imperative to act against the harm resulting from globalization derives not from any guilt over how the community has benefited, but from Judaism's bottom-line, iconoclastic monotheism.

"My tradition doesn't tell me to fight globalization, because globalization is in and of itself bad, but it does tell me to look at globalization and to decide, based on my observation, whether globalization is building a world of more love and compassion and respect for the sacred, or whether it is doing the opposite," says Lerner. "There is nothing in Torah that relates directly to globalization. But if globalization is just the latest twist on the worship of materialism, then it has become idolatry, the antithesis of monotheism, and that, my tradition tells me, is to be opposed."

Globalization, says Lerner, "has great potential as a concept." A world in which critical information and limited resources are shared, and in which democracy and human rights are given greater respect, is of benefit to all. Globalization's "reality" is another matter, however, and that is because it lacks a concurrent "globalization of spirit."

Spirituality, as explained by Lerner, "is a lived experience, a set of practices and a consciousness that aligns us with a sense of the sanctity of All Being." Among spirituality's defining traits are the experience of "love and connection to the world and to others," recognition of the underlying unity between all life and the planet, and "conviction that the universe is not negative or neutral but tilts toward goodness and love."[11]

A place to begin cultivating spirituality is celebration of the Sabbath, Judaism's corrective for the tyranny of the marketplace, says Lerner. Sabbath observance is a pillar of traditional Judaism, one of the Ten Commandments. Jews are enjoined by scripture to cease all work-related activities on the Sabbath because that's what God did following the Creation. "And God blessed the seventh day and made it holy because He ceased in it from doing all His work, which God had created" (Genesis 2:3).

The Jewish Sabbath traditionally runs from sundown Friday to sundown Saturday (Hebrew calendar days start at sundown in line with Genesis's counting of Creation's first week). The Sabbath is a suspension of time. It's a day set aside for reflection, prayer, rest, and the healing company of loved ones. Lerner suggests that observing the Sabbath helps one break free of the sort of all-consuming corporate mentality that fuels globalization's negative aspects.

Waskow, with whom Lerner has often worked closely over the years, adds two other ancient practices of Judaism as antidotes for globalization's compulsive self-centeredness and consumption. The first is the Sabbatical Year—the biblically mandated year of rest for the land. Every seven years, according to Leviticus, the land of Israel is supposed to remain untended and allowed to regenerate itself through rest (the Sabbatical Year, *shemittah* in Hebrew, is still observed in highly modified form in Israel). Reliance upon God rather than upon the labors of humanity is stressed. Debts are to be cancelled as an extension of the Sabbath desire to free the spirit from commercial taint.

Waskow is under no illusion that global economic interests will cease their incessant activity and allow the natural environment to remain undisturbed for a full year, or that the Sabbatical Year has any practical application in a world with too many hungry mouths clamoring for food. Moreover, the Sabbatical Year, as with virtually all Jewish law, was meant to apply to Jews alone. The point, he says, is to use the Sabbatical Year concept to raise awareness among Jews and others about the growing environmental degradation that has been hastened by the globalization of resource extraction by distant multinational corporations.

The second ancient practice Waskow advocates is Jubilee—a concept successfully seized upon by the international debt-reduction movement in 2000. The ancient Israelites marked Jubilee every fifty years, upon the completion of seven Sabbatical Year cycles. The intention was to provide a new start for the poor by recycling the community's wealth. Land sold since the previous Jubilee reverted to its original owner—which meant the family that had received the plot following the initial conquest of the land of Canaan by the Joshua-led Israelite tribes. Moreover, all slaves were to be freed and given a grant to help establish themselves. "If applied perfectly, these provisions would insure that no individual amassed excessive wealth, nor would any Jew be reduced to perpetual poverty and servitude," the *Encyclopedia of Judaism* explains.[12]

Jubilee also was intended for Jews only, and then only for when the original twelve Israelite tribes were intact and inhabiting the land of Israel. As a result, the practice disappeared with the start of the Babylonian exile—almost 2,500 years ago. Despite that, Waskow believes Jubilee can serve as a motivating metaphor for restoring economic justice, even in a globalized, overwhelmingly non-Jewish world. In fact, that's just what happened with Jubilee 2000, a campaign embraced by Roman Catholic, Protestant, and other non-Jewish religious leaders, as well as governments and secular human rights groups. It resulted in the forgiving of billions of dollars in international debt owed by some of the world's poorest nations who, because they had no ability to pay back the loans on their own, were beholden to global banking entities.

Tikkun olam is Judaism's term for working to improve the world. Kabbalah, Judaism's mystical branch, teaches that the Jewish destiny is to continually engage in tikkun olam to help usher in some distant messianic conclusion. Tikkun olam means that humans and God are partners in the fate of the world—God cannot achieve full justice without human assistance. It is an utter rejection of fatalism and the embracing of eternal hope. Here's Waskow relating tikkun olam to today's global economic order:

> The criticism of globalization is not an attack on capitalism per se. The Torah, in fact, affirms the acquisition of wealth. So Torah is not capitalist or socialist. It is only anti-capitalism run amuck or

anti-socialism run amuck. In Jewish thought we are all accountable to God, and so we are obligated to help right the wrong that corporations that seem accountable to no one are leaving in their wake. Globalization is a threat to everyone, Jews and non-Jews, and we need to educate people so that they understand that an underpaid, exploited worker in China hurts someone in Detroit by denying them a job at a wage that while higher is only fair given the return to the corporation. That is our job, our role. That, too, is repairing the world's soul.

Globalization, many would say, is a given. Corporations have achieved global reach and global power, cultures can no longer easily remain aloof from each other, and even harsh critics of the process travel to protests around the world on transcontinental airliners carrying cell phones and bank cards that work in scores of nations. What is left to resist? Is criticism of globalization simply an effort to smooth some of its rougher edges? Michael Lerner, drawing on the model of Judaism, answers this last question with a resounding "no."

The faith's central message, he says, is that God is not only a God of justice but is also a God of eternal hope. "There is a force in the universe that makes possible 'what ought to be' out of 'what is.' To believe in the God of Judaism is to reject today's reality for tomorrow's possibility," he says. "God is the power of transformation in the universe. It's the voice of the future urging us to become better for ourselves and for the world. Jewish spirituality is the cultivation of this attitude of hope."

Talking with Michael Feinberg in his lower Manhattan office, just blocks from where the World Trade Center once stood, I asked him whether he ever loses hope, whether fighting corporate giants day in and day out ever leaves him limp. Is the fight against corporate globalization quixotic?

A sober accounting of the wins and losses would argue against hope, he replied. Yet in the depths of his Jewish soul, there also lives the messianic spark articulated by Lerner. "My intellect says there is no hope, but my heart says devote your life to change," Feinberg says.

And so he continues to speak his truth to power. It is, after all, Judaism's essential ethical teaching, and its prophetic tradition.

5

Buddhism:
BODHISATTVAS IN BOARDROOMS

IN THE CLASSIC STORY OF HIS ENLIGHTENMENT, Siddhartha Gautama, the Sakya prince who came to be called the Buddha, is said to have realized the nature of reality during a night of meditation beneath the sheltering limbs of the bodhi tree. First he remembered his past lives. Next he recognized the nature of cause and effect—*karma*. Then he clarified the way to end dissatisfaction. Ever since, the "Awakened One" has most often been depicted in meditative poses, and Buddhism has been portrayed as a spiritual discipline concerned more with inner process than with worldly involvement.

There is some truth in this characterization. In its Asian homelands, Buddhist practice has often been more about gaining personal merit than about communal responsibility. David R. Loy, an American Buddhist scholar who teaches at Japan's Bunkyo University, criticizes this tendency in a recent essay:

Rural Thailand, for example, needs more hospitals and clinics more than it needs new temples. According to the popular view, however, a wealthy person gains more merit by funding the construction of a temple—whether or not one already exists in that area. Such a narrow but commonplace understanding of *dana* [generosity] as merit-making has worked well to provide for the *sangha* [the religious community], but cannot be an adequate spiritual response to the challenges provided by globalization.[1]

Sybille Scholz, executive director of the Buddhist Peace Fellowship in Berkeley, California, adds that some traditional Buddhists, Asian and non-Asian, question whether serious Buddhist practice leaves any room at all for political involvement. "They would say it soils the purity of intention. But I think that things are changing in Asia and elsewhere. More Buddhist religious leaders are becoming aware of the impact they can have as religious leaders on political issues. They see it happening elsewhere, among Catholic liberation theology activists, for example, and they follow suit," says the German-born Scholz, who came to Buddhism following involvement in environmental and human rights work.

The world has changed, for Buddhists as it has for others, and the observations of Loy and Scholz are acknowledgment of that fact. Globalization has forced its way into Buddhist lands (where it's often eagerly embraced) and Buddhist practice has migrated to the West. Transnational

companies do business in Thailand and Vietnam, and originate in Japan. Tibetan Buddhist centers flourish in Nova
Scotia and Brazil. The smiling face of Tenzin Gyatso, four-
teenth in a line of Tibetan spiritual and political leaders each
known as the Dalai Lama, graces Manhattan billboards.
"Prospective Buddhist practitioners can find virtually every
Buddhist sect, from every Asian Buddhist tradition, present
on the North American continent," says Buddhist historian
Charles S. Prebish.[2]

Some 2,500 years have passed since the Buddha's
night of insights, and it would be a mistake to speak today
of Buddhism as a monolithic tradition. Buddhist sectarian-
ism became widespread within several hundred years of the
Buddha's death with a proliferation of sects and subsects
accompanying the tradition's geographic advance across
Asia. It is possible, however, to speak of core values that
transcend this sectarian-
ism, and it is these values,
despite variance in their
execution, that inform the
general Buddhist response
to globalization.

A starting point is the
central tenet concerning
the interconnectedness
of all life—the "Indra's
Web" of Buddhist (by way
of Hindu) mythology.
Buddhism teaches that literally everything under

Rather than focusing on economic growth, Buddhism maintains that the public welfare is
best served through individual
attention to the practice of generosity and compassion. Buddhists say sharing creates bonds
between individuals and stifles
personal greed, and that concern for others encourages reciprocity and the sense of
interdependence. Individual spiritual growth, in short, promotes
communal advancement.

the sun, from plankton to people and even the sun itself, are elements of one interconnected whole, a latticelike web in which each luminous jewel of creation reflects all others, fostering interdependence and interaction. Call it primal globalization—the organic origin of today's economic and cultural globalization.

Thich Nhat Hanh, the well-known Vietnamese Zen teacher and peace activist, coined the term "interbeing" to explain this Buddhist understanding. Interbeing, he says, rejects all notions of separateness, all notions of permanence apart from the web of interconnected relationships. "When we look at green vegetables, we should know that it is the sun that is green and not just the vegetables. The green color in the leaves of the vegetables is due to the presence of the sun. Without the sun, no living being could survive. Without sun, water, air and soil, there would be no vegetables. The vegetables are the coming-together of many conditions near and far."[3]

Buddhist ethical teachings emphasize that this interdependence comes with a moral component. For humans, that means maintaining a sense of universal responsibility in all endeavors. Here's what the current Dalai Lama, arguably the world's best-known Buddhist, says on the issue:

> A stock-market crash on one side of the globe can have a direct effect on the economies of countries on the other. Similarly, our technological achievements are now such that our activities have an unambiguous effect on the natural environment. And the very size of our population means that we

cannot any longer afford to ignore others' interests.... In view of this, I am convinced that it is
essential that we cultivate a sense of what I call universal responsibility.[4]

Buddhist tradition holds that the Buddha himself for-
mulated the progression of insights known as the Four
Noble Truths. The first truth is that of suffering. From the
pain of childbirth to the inevitability of death, all people, to
varying degrees, experience loss, grief, and despair. The second truth is that the human craving to avoid suffering is,
paradoxically, at the very root of our suffering, and the
third truth is that it is possible to eliminate the craving
through the awareness offered by a transformed mind. The
fourth truth is the Eightfold Path, the Buddhist formula of
practices for cultivating the transformation that leads to
the extinction of craving and suffering.

Included in the Eightfold Path is "right livelihood." In
traditional Buddhist society, that meant avoiding occupa-
tions that involved killing, such as hunting or the butcher-
ing of livestock (additional prohibitions applied to monks
and nuns). But right livelihood is also interpreted to
demand ethical behavior in business dealings, not only
because of the need to avoid harming others—remember
the Dalai Lama's statement about universal responsibility—
but also to avoid doing harm to oneself. Both are viewed as
impediments to personal spiritual development.

Buddhist critics have made right livelihood a cornerstone of their argument against the manner in which globalization has unfolded.

For more than three decades, Les Kaye toiled in the

Silicon Valley corporate world, working in various administrative and technical positions for the global information
technology giant IBM. But he mixed his nine-to-five life
with a commitment to Soto Zen, a Japanese Buddhist tradition. In 1990, Kaye left IBM for full-time Zen practice;
today he is the abbot of Kannon Do, a Zen center in
Mountain View, California.

Kaye agrees with the importance of discerning what
constitutes right livelihood. But he's quick to add that in the
relative world of daily existence, separating right from wrong
livelihood can be as tough a personal decision as a Buddhist
may ever confront. Kaye notes the eagerness with which
Buddhist nations have sought to grab globalization's gold
ring in an attempt to provide life's basic physical needs for
burgeoning populations. The price they pay is steep in terms
of communal and environmental stability, and corruption
often limits any benefits for the masses, Kaye adds. But do
not think that alternative systems are easily substituted, and
do not forget the greater difficulty that powerless individuals,
Buddhists or otherwise, face when their children must eat.

"The Buddha and his monks did not have to support
families and did not have to make this moral decision," says
Kaye. "Life isn't so simple anymore for the lay practitioner
who has that responsibility, not in Asia or anywhere else,
and lay practice pretty much defines Buddhism as it has
evolved in the West."

Kaye's practical formulation is in keeping with his
Buddhist perspective; critical observation reveals a subtle
truth that defies easy pronouncements. There is no black
and white, merely shades of gray. Categorization is an illu-

sion; never forget the need for compassion. And watch out for greed, *lobha*, one of Buddhism's "three poisons," or roots of evil, and the impetus, says Kaye, behind globalization's delusional insistence that big is better and bigger is better yet. The Buddhist way runs counter.

Economist E. F. Schumacher was not a Buddhist, although he was heavily influenced by Buddhist thought, yet he summed up the Buddhist way nicely with his spare but elegant pronouncement that "small is beautiful." The economic system advocated in his classic 1973 book *Small Is Beautiful: Economics As If People Mattered*, drew on his understanding of right livelihood in combination with his beliefs about the efficacy and moral superiority of localized, cooperative, and sustainable economic systems.[5]

Buddhist skeptics of globalization have adopted Schumacher's critique in the absence of any direct teachings on economics in the Buddhist canon. They note that economic globalism—offspring of the free-market capitalism Schumacher regarded as deeply flawed—fosters greed, competitiveness, and consumerism, all of which are in contradiction to the Buddhist values of generosity, compassion, nonattachment, community, and a deep respect for the natural world.

"The most important point, from a Buddhist perspective, is that our economic emphasis on competition, individual gain, and private possession encourages the development of ill will rather than loving-kindness," David R. Loy says of the globalized economy. "A society where people do not feel that they benefit from sharing with each other has already begun to break down."[6]

Kenneth Kraft, a scholar of Japanese Zen who teaches at Lehigh University in Pennsylvania, adds another point. Buddhism, he says, advises discernment between needs and desires. Globalized capitalism "seems to scream desire...Buddhism would argue for less consumption and more joy" by recognizing unnecessary consumption as desire, and then engaging in the practices that allow you to resist succumbing to it. "It's the idea of the immediate *sangha* taking precedence over growth for growth's sake, eating a local potato versus getting one from overseas."

Rather than emphasizing social justice in a Western sense, Buddhism maintains that the public welfare is served through individual attention to the practice of generosity and compassion. Sharing creates bonds between individuals and stifles personal greed. Concern for others encourages reciprocity and the sense of interdependence. Individual spiritual growth, in short, promotes communal advancement.[7]

Yet Buddhism is hardly static (isn't the abiding belief in impermanence the tradition's hallmark?), and cultural globalization involves much cross-pollination. Globalization has eased the way for Buddhism to gain a solid foothold in the West, but it has also given Western Buddhists the opportunity to impose some of their own values on their adopted path. Women and the laity have far greater roles among Western Buddhists than they enjoy in historically Buddhist lands, for example. But perhaps a more relevant development is the adaptation of the belief in social justice as understood in the Abrahamic traditions (Judaism, Christianity, and Islam), which regard it as a divine entitlement that must be rigorously defended. Western Buddhist converts may have dropped the divine entitlement part, but they've stayed true to their belief in the necessity for direct action on behalf of social justice causes. They call it "engaged Buddhism," and they've made it a path for opposition to the ills they see in economic globalization.

If "small is beautiful" stands in for Buddhist economics, then engaged Buddhism summarizes a newly articulated political code. One of its more eloquent proponents is Robert Aitken Roshi, founder of Honolulu's Diamond Sangha, cofounder of the Buddhist Peace Fellowship, and one of the most highly respected of Western Zen Buddhists.

"I suggest that it is...time for us to take ourselves in hand. We ourselves can establish and engage in the very policies and programs of social and ecological protection and respect that we have heretofore so futilely demanded from authorities," he says. "This would be engaged Buddhism, where the sangha is not merely parallel to the forms of conventional society and not merely metaphysical in its universality."[8]

Kraft says engaged Buddhism "for the first time in human history" offers a "charged vision" of "the deep spirituality of Asia fused with the social transformation of the West.... Perhaps Buddhist reflection will enable Western-style action to become a little less mechanical.... I think engaged Buddhism might also help Westerners gain greater understanding of the suffering of others, because Buddhism insists upon looking at the reality of a situation, whereas too often in the West people want to fix things just to make unpleasantness disappear."

Western Buddhist converts have integrated their belief in the necessity for direct action on behalf of social justice causes into their practice. Inspired by Vietnamese activist, teacher, and writer Thich Nhat Hanh and others, they call it "engaged Buddhism." Engaged Buddhists may be found working in inner-city homeless shelters and AIDS hospices, or demonstrating against military adventurism and environmental exploitation. When they do demonstrate, though, Western engaged Buddhists seek to make a statement by their *presence*, rather than by their *action*.

Engaged Buddhists may be found working in inner-city homeless shelters and AIDS hospices, or demonstrating against military adventurism and environmental exploitation. When they do demonstrate, though, Western engaged Buddhists seek to make a statement by their *presence*, rather than their *action*. It's a subtle distinction, but one that's critical to understanding the Buddhist approach.

"We're the ones who protest quietly," explains Scholz of the Buddhist Peace Fellowship. "Holding up signs and making noise is like spitting in the wind. You impact no one because you are dismissed for your aggressiveness. And, besides, it makes you a more aggressive person, which just feeds into more aggressive action the next time you decide to protest. We try and be quiet. Silence allows space for listening. It opens up a space for dialogue that can be trusted," says Scholz, whose organization calls itself a catalyst for "progressive social change."

Engaged Buddhism's primary relevance to globalism is in its criticism of the underlying economic and political mindsets that are seen as advancing the process of global-ization by encouraging ever-greater profit margins and by deifying consumerism. And while it is, in the main, a Western phenomenon, engaged Buddhism is by no means restricted to Western Buddhists.

In Thailand, a Buddhist nation that has been both swamped and seduced by economic and cultural global-ization, Sulak Sivaraksa has emerged as one of engaged Buddhism's leading international voices. A longtime lay activist who touts Buddhist virtues as a cure for the ills of globalization that he believes have ravaged Siam—the his-torical, and his preferred, name for Thailand—Sivaraksa identifies imported Western materialism as the cause of his homeland's wholesale abandonment of its traditional values. He points out that the process has been going on for more than a century and a half, or ever since King Mongkut—a posthumously global figure himself thanks to his portrayal in *The King and I*—succumbed to pressure and opened his nation to Western trade. However enter-taining the Broadway show's music, the process has left his homeland awash in sex tourism, Coca Cola, and unregu-lated capitalist nightmares. Buddhism, Sivaraksa laments, has been reduced to Siam's state religion, with no more hold on the general population than the Church of England has on British football rowdies. Globalists hype technology as being key to future breakthroughs, but Sivaraksa questions its implications for a truly Buddhist society. He is no Luddite—he makes wide use of the Web to spread his message, for example. Sivaraksa's point is that technical prowess must be considered in relationship.

Again, nothing stands apart. Every action has its consequences, and awareness of negative consequences divides right from questionable livelihood.

"Is advanced technology contrary to Buddhist values? In one way I think it is," Sivaraksa says. "People speak about technology as if it were value-free, when in fact it is not. The metaphysical assumption of technology is that man is a supreme being. Man can destroy anything in the name of progress. Most importantly, advanced technology belongs to a development path that pays no attention to the needs of people. Robots may produce faster, but they create human unemployment. This is contrary to human and Buddhist values."[9]

So far in this chapter I have focused on the opinions of Buddhists who at a minimum view globalization with enormous trepidation. But I also noted that there is no one Buddhism, that the tradition is not monolithic. A differing attitude toward globalization is exhibited by Soka Gakkai Buddhists. While also critical of globalism's darker aspects and identifying itself as within the engaged Buddhist tent, the Soka Gakkai movement has surfed the globalization wave to establish itself in more than 160 nations. Along the way it has gained a place at the table around which the international elite gather to debate a global ethic for the new world order. That includes official nongovernmental organization status at the United Nations for Soka Gakkai International, the movement's corporate umbrella, and whose very name reflects its global perspective.

Soka Gakkai (translated from Japanese as the Society for the Creation of Value) claims some twelve million members worldwide and is the largest lay Buddhist movement in the United States, claiming 300,000 adherents. Moreover, it is the only one in the nation that has attracted large numbers of racial minorities to its ranks.[10]

Soka Gakkai (once known as Nichiren Shoshu) is a modern phenomenon, having been founded as a social reform movement in Japan in 1930. However, its roots may be traced to the thirteenth-century Japanese Buddhist priest Nichiren Daishonin, who proclaimed his interpretation the true Buddhism, a formulation that to this day breeds distance between Soka Gakkai and other sects that followed his path and the remainder of the Buddhist world. In North America, for example, that often translates into limited cooperation between Western converts to Soka Gakkai and equally recent converts to Zen, Vipassana, or Tibetan Buddhist practices.

Soka Gakkai—independent since a nasty power struggle that led to a 1991 break with its former Japanese priestly overlords—is a practical-minded faith that presents itself as a humanistic path offering optimism and direction to the average person. Its members pray for personal benefits and its spirit is forward looking, extroverted, and socially tolerant— qualities that have enabled it to open easily to the tenor of global-village enthusiasts.

"Soka Gakkai Buddhism is an essentially this-worldly rather than an other-worldly religion, with a concept of salvation relevant to the here and now rather than to the hereafter," says Bryan Wilson, the eminent Oxford University religion scholar. "Unlike many other Buddhist organizations," Wilson notes, "members are not enjoined to relinquish involvement in the world; on the contrary, their participation in civic, political, artistic, cultural, and social activities is positively endorsed. The 'world-denying' attitude of ascetic religions is altogether remote from the perspective on life espoused by this variant of Buddhism.... The teachings of the movement promote a view of religion as an instrument of benefit, not as a compensation for suffering."[11]

Soka Gakkai worship is focused on the *Lotus Sutra,* an early and revered Buddhist canon that for Soka Gakkai Buddhists contains all essential truths. The primary practice is repetitive chanting of *nam-myoho-renge-kyo,* the title of the Lotus Sutra, while seated before the *Gohonzon,* a scroll that includes Lotus Sutra passages. Nichiren Buddhism is highly popular in Japan, where it has also backed its own political party and been quite controversial.

Soka Gakkai, the largest lay Buddhist movement in the United States, is in the forefront of Buddhist groups directly addressing globalization's problems. Founded in Japan, it is a practical-minded faith that presents itself as a humanistic path offering optimism and direction to the average person. Its members pray for personal benefits and its spirit is forward looking, extroverted, and socially tolerant—qualities that have enabled it to open easily to the tenor of global-village enthusiasts.

Yet for all its theological and stylistic differences, Soka Gakkai takes note of the same Buddhist core values that Buddhists more suspicious of globalization also profess—the unity of all life, the need for individual change to precede communal advancement, the connection between personal satisfaction and helping others gain their satisfaction. Under the Soka Gakkai banner, members engage in civic improvement and cultural and educational projects around the world. The organization's literature is replete with references to working for world peace, environmental protection, public education, and human rights. Soka Gakkai's biggest project is seeking to influence globalization's course.

A major step toward that goal came in 1993, when Soka Gakkai founded the Boston Research Center for the 21st Century, an "international peace institute" for fostering scholarly dialogue across national, cultural, and religious boundaries. The hope is to create a global ethic sensitive to globalism's manifest problems—economic inequities, environmental exploitation, negation of traditional spiritual and cultural values, and human rights violations.

"We don't see ourselves as promoting Buddhism, but rather Buddhist humanism," says Valerie Straus, the center's executive director. "What's needed is a globalization of an ethical consciousness that can help guide other forms of globalization, which at this point are out ahead of any changed sense of values or consciousness.... We believe in dialogue rather than the use of force. People aren't born pacifists; they're taught to be pacifists. Likewise, people aren't born to be terrorists; they're taught to be terrorists. How we educate people is therefore key to having the kind of society we want. We hope to be a beacon of light helping to point the way."

Bodhisattva is the Sanskrit Buddhist term for someone whose compassionate qualities are said to be so acute

that they have postponed their own enlightenment in order
to help others gain that state (the Dalai Lama is traditionally believed to be such a being). Daisaku Ikeda, the president of Soka Gakkai International, has recast this ancient
and complex concept in light of globalization. Ikeda speaks
of bodhisattvas as world citizens who work for the benefit
of all. "My dream is to see all the world's religious and cultural traditions produce a continuous stream of such world
citizens who will compete with one another to contribute to
world peace," he says.[12]

Ikeda's use of the term in so modern a context raises a
few traditional eyebrows. Yet his underlying point is strict-
ly traditional: compassion toward others is the critical difference between selfishness and selflessness, between
world conflict and harmony. In this, Ikeda is in complete
agreement with the Dalai Lama.

Compassion, says the Dalai Lama, "breaks down barriers of every kind and in the end destroys the notion of my
interest as independent from others' interest. But most
important, so far as ethics is concerned, where love of one's
neighbor, affection, kindness, and compassion live, we find
that ethical conduct is automatic. Ethically wholesome
actions arise naturally in the context of compassion."[13]

Ikeda and the Dalai Lama represent two seemingly
disparate faces of contemporary Buddhism. The former is
Japanese and wears western business suits; the latter is a
Tibetan who wears the ochre and maroon robes of a monk.
Their approaches and life experiences vary greatly, yet both
are global figures that hold dear their tradition's essential
spiritual truths. Buddhism's version of unity in diversity is

at play here as well, and the Buddhist consensus concerning globalization is made clear.

Globalization, says that vision, must be made to serve
the many rather than the few, and the need for inner
process does not negate the need for outer action on behalf
of those who are not being served. It's a matter of enlight-
ened self-interest and even if hugging isn't your thing, don't
forget the trees. Because they too are us, as is everything.

6

Bahá'í Faith:
ONE FOR ALL

ALONG WITH THE TALLEST TREE, the person with the longest hair, and the world's best-selling chocolate candy, the *Guinness Book of World Records* lists the City Montessori School (CMS) of Lucknow, India, as the world's largest single-city, private educational institution. The City Montessori School has almost 26,000 students in preschool through college-level programs, a distinction earned through its reputation for academic excellence and strict attention to moral education. However, CMS is noteworthy for another reason: its curriculum is designed to prepare students for a world in which globalization is considered God's will.

"The creator is one, and all the manifestations of God have come from the one source. Lord Rama, Moses, Jesus, Muhammad—all from the same source to share ethical teachings that never change," says CMS cofounder Jagdish Gandhi. "Wholeness is God's plan in every way, and globalism is the wholeness God has planned for us for this age."

The City Montessori School presents itself as a secular institution open to members of all religions—its student body is 70 percent Hindu, 25 percent Muslim, and 5 percent Christian and Sikh. But there's no mistaking from where the CMS emphasis on globalism derives. Gandhi is a Bahá'í, and CMS is a functional expression of his belief in the spiritual and global unity that lies at the core of the faith's religious teachings. "We live the life of the Bahá'í," Gandhi says of himself and his wife, Bharti, with whom he cofounded CMS in 1959. "We don't force our teachers or students to be Bahá'ís. We just live the life, but we see it does influence them."

Many religions see themselves as *the* universal vehicle for salvation. However, none identifies so unambiguously with globalization as the path to worldly salvation as does the Bahá'í Faith, which claims some 5 million adherents from more than 2,100 ethnic groups living in some 235 nations and territories. Bahá'ís say they have the world's most dispersed and ethnically diverse religious organization. Not only does this lay-led, clergyless tradition preach globalization, it embodies it.

Shoghi Effendi, the faith's "Guardian," or administrative leader, for nearly four decades until his death in 1957, explained the faith's perspective on globalism as follows:

> Unification of the whole of mankind is the hallmark of the state which human society is now approaching. Unity of family, of tribe, of city-state and nation have been successively attempted and fully established. World unity is the goal towards which a

harassed humanity is striving. Nation-building has come to an end. The anarchy inherent in state sovereignty is moving towards a climax. A world, growing to maturity, must abandon this fetish, recognize the oneness and wholeness of human relationships, and establish once and for all the machinery that can best incarnate this fundamental principle of its life.[1]

For Bahá'ís, then, globalization is both inevitable and welcome as God's spiritual plan for individual and world salvation. Think of it as monotheism writ large. Think of the Bahá'í system of local and regional elected governing councils culminating in its overarching Universal House of Justice as an executive blueprint for organizing and administering globalism's inexorable triumph.

At CMS, the Gandhis view the education of young people as the best way to prepare the groundwork for the vision articulated by Effendi. "Education is God's way of changing society," says Jagdish Gandhi, who adopted the

> For Bahá'ís, globalization is both inevitable and welcome as God's spiritual plan for individual and world salvation. Bahá'ís see the world as a reflection of God's unity. They believe that humanity will at some future but undetermined date accede to:
> - one world language
> - one world parliament
> - one executive body
> - one world tribunal
> - one world "Force" for maintaining order
> - one world metropolis that will serve as the global "nerve center"

last name of India's prophet of nonviolent revolution, Mahatma Gandhi, out of respect. "Everything we do at CMS is designed to foster global thinking."

Indeed. Telephone the school and you'll hear the Disney tune "It's a Small World" play over and over as you wait on hold. Students wear outfits festooned with the symbols of world religions and various national flags as they sing songs of peace. International student exchanges and academic competitions are the order of the day. "CMS was established by my wife and myself with the objective of realizing our goal of world unity and world peace by raising a new generation of world citizens," says Jagdish.

"It is no longer possible to live in isolation of each other," he continues, quoting his own Web site. "The sooner we recognize this, the more we can prepare our children for the future. CMS's education system strives to break down the existing narrow domestic walls and to open up new possibilities for global cooperation in all fields of human endeavor."[2]

Bahá'ís see the world as a reflection of God's unity. They believe that humanity will at some future but undetermined date accede to one world language, one world parliament, one executive body, one world tribunal, one world "Force" for maintaining order, and one world metropolis that will serve as the global "nerve center." And it will all mirror the Bahá'í Faith's own tight-knit and hierarchical corporate structure that is designed to forestall any possibility of schism, which is seen as the antithesis of unity and the reason why other religions have failed to fulfill their earthly tasks. Bahá'ís, to quote Effendi once again, foresee a "world commonwealth in which all nations, races, creeds and classes are closely and permanently united, and in which the autonomy of its state members and the personal freedom and initiative of the individuals that compose them are definitely and completely safeguarded."[3] (The Bahá'í penchant for unity is backed up by threatening dissidents with a form of excommunication that includes shunning by family members and friends. However, Bahá'í leaders insist this in no way conflicts with the promise to safeguard personal freedom.)

The Bahá'í proclivity for globalization is rooted in the formative writings of its founder, Bahá'u'lláh ("Glory of God"), a nineteenth-century Persian religious leader who declared himself the latest (but not the last) of the one God's prophets—"Messengers" in the Bahá'í lexicon—that, as Jagdish Gandhi notes, includes Abraham, Moses, Buddha, Zoroaster, Jesus, Muhammad, and others. Humans, wrote Bahá'u'lláh, "have been created to carry forward an ever-advancing civilization."[4]

Bahá'u'lláh taught that humankind's social and spiritual evolution proceed along complementary paths, that there exists a prevailing unity within humanity's seemingly endless diversity, and that the human journey involves the creation of ever more complex and efficient systems for attaining moral and material progress. Globalism, for all its faults—and Bahá'ís recognize and work toward alleviating many—is seen as this era's contribution to the ever-evolving human drama.

Just as its origins in the Abrahamic tradition—and in staunchly monotheistic Islam in particular—explain the unstinting Bahá'í emphasis on the unity of all things, the faith's relatively recent arrival, coming as it did well into the modern age, helps explain its classical liberal analysis of the contemporary condition. Earlier religious manifestations are regarded as also divinely inspired but reflecting less-developed stages of human social organization. But unlike liberal secular critics who view human development as having outgrown organized faith, Bahá'ís see religion as God's plan for achieving a peaceful and just global order.

"The process of integrating human beings into larger and larger groups, although influenced by culture and geography, has been driven largely by religion, the most powerful agent for changing human attitudes and behavior," the faith's international Office of Public Information states in a 1995 document. "By religion, however, we mean the essential foundation or reality of religion, not the dogmas and blind imitations which have gradually encrusted it and which are the cause of its decline and effacement."[5]

Bahá'ís are enjoined by their faith from engaging in partisan politics, which they view as inherently divisive and contrary to the quest for unity (they are allowed to vote, however, which keeps them out of trouble in nations where voting is mandatory). Likewise, they refrain from public political debate and adversarial protest and stress obedience to civil law. That does not mean they shy away from seeking to influence government decisions, even as they believe the system of nation-states to be inching toward its inevitable dissolve. The preferred Bahá'í arena is the very world in which the debate over globalization is most advanced—the international arena populated by think tanks, nongovernmental agencies, and cooperative governmental bodies. Dedicated Bahá'ís are attracted to this global village by the promise of helping to actualize Bahá'u'lláh's worldview. It's an example of putting into practice Bahá'u'lláh's teaching that work performed in service of others is in itself a form of worshipping God. Moreover, Bahá'u'lláh also urged creation of a mechanism for global governance, and Bahá'ís see in organizations such as the League of Nations and the United Nations (UN) a foreshadowing of their perfected world to come.

The hope that Bahá'ís place in the mission and ability of the UN is evident in this optimistic statement—some might say overly so given the United Nations' inability to achieve so many of its stated goals—from the Bahá'í International Community Office of Public Information: "In the stunned aftermath of World War II, far-sighted leaders found it at last possible, through the United Nations organization, to begin consolidating the foundations of world order. Long dreamed of by progressive thinkers, the new system of international conventions and related agencies was now endowed with crucial powers that had tragically been denied to the abortive League of Nations."[6]

Bahá'ís walk a fine line at the UN between program advocacy and avoiding taking sides in international disagreements. One conflict they do involve themselves in is supporting passage of annual UN resolutions condemning the persecution of Iranian Bahá'ís (Iran is the successor state to ancient Persia), who are reviled as heretics by Teheran's conservative Muslim rulers because of Bahá'u'lláh's claim to being a prophet who followed Muhammad, the final prophet as far as Islam is concerned. A 2000 U.S. State Department report notes Iranian government policies that "appear to be geared to destroying [Bahá'ís] as a community. Bahá'ís repeatedly have been offered relief from oppression if they were prepared to recant their faith."[7]

Bahá'ís were on hand for the United Nations' 1945 founding in San Francisco, and since 1948 have had international observer status as a nongovernmental organization (NGO). Over the years, the faith has gained consultative status with the UN Economic and Social Council and the United Nations Children's Fund (UNICEF). Bahá'ís also work with such UN-related agencies as the World Health Organization, the United Nations Environment Program, and the United Nations Development Fund for Women. In 2000, Techeste Ahderom, a native of Eritrea who at the time ran the Bahá'í UN office, became the first NGO representative to address the world body's General Assembly.

Bani Dugal is the current head of the Bahá'í UN office in New York. Her work, she says, is an extension of her Bahá'í beliefs. "I am a diplomat for my faith, although we don't outwardly teach our faith at the UN. We are promoting the principles on which we believe there can be world peace."

Outside Iran, most Bahá'ís adopted the religion as adults after being attracted by its utopian ideals. The Gandhis, for example, who run the City Montessori School, became Bahá'ís some fifteen years after founding CMS. Jagdish Gandhi said he and his wife converted from Hinduism after meeting Bahá'í students at an international conference in London in 1974 and being impressed by their "spiritual purpose." In the 1960s, sizeable numbers of white American liberals and African Americans (jazz musician Dizzy Gillespie included) imbued with the era's spirit of radical social change joined the movement. Dugal also came to the faith as an adult.

Born into a Sikh family in India, Dugal initially encountered Bahá'í beliefs after moving to the United States. Sikhism is a South Asian faith with its own emphasis on monotheistic unity and social equality, all of which predisposed Dugal toward Bahá'í teachings. But Bahá'í theology held an added attraction for her she felt lacking in Sikhism, and that was the Bahá'í emphasis on gender equality.

Bahá'í leaders stress the emphasis on gender equality, despite the all-male character of the faith's highest administrative body, the Universal House of Justice, whose exclusion of women was dictated by Bahá'u'lláh. Like other Bahá'ís, Dugal says she accepts the male-only rule as an unexplainable article of faith, despite its obvious contradiction with professed Bahá'í policy. More important to her is the gender equality Bahá'ís practice at other levels of daily life, and which she regards as essential for true social justice. Dugal says that became clear to her while working as an attorney in India, where she often represented women clients within a patriarchal legal system. That and a growing sense that global cooperation was needed to end continuing world conflict convinced her to become a Bahá'í.

Dugal has been working at the Bahá'í UN office since 1994, four years after she "declared" herself a member of the Faith, which took place in a simple ceremony during which belief in Bahá'u'lláh and his teachings was stated.

"Becoming a Bahá'í helped me define the direction I was already headed. I was drawn to the international stage by inclination. It was an affirmation of who I had become," she says. Dugal recognizes the United Nations' imperfections. Her quest is to move the world body in the direction of what Bahá'ís refer to as "consultation."

"The Bahá'í concept of consultation is certainly different than what is practiced at the United Nations, where what is looked for above all is consensus," she says. "Consultation for a Bahá'í is to enter into discussions free of preconceived notions and with a belief that the truth will emerge during the process of discussion and not because of politics or deal making, and that the truth will benefit all. We attempt to do this at the United Nations when meeting with NGOs and governments, to get them to move toward recognizing other viewpoints and let go of their preconceived notions. But it would be dishonest to say that we are able to gain that effect, but that clearly is the goal."

A similar interest in global cooperation also shaped W. Andy Knight's professional and religious thinking. As a child growing up in Barbados, his first exposure to life beyond his Caribbean island-nation home came via the British Broadcasting Corporation. His nascent

Since 1948 Bahá'ís have had international observer status as a nongovernmental organization at the United Nations. Bani Dugal is the current head of the Bahá'í UN office in New York. Her work, she says, is an extension of her Bahá'í beliefs. She considers herself to be a diplomat for her faith, promoting the principles on which Bahá'ís believe there can be world peace.

interest in international affairs was further nurtured by listening in on conversations between his father, a Pentecostal Christian minister, and a family friend, who happened to be Barbados's UN ambassador. When the time came to choose a college, Knight left for Canada, intent on a career focused on multinational issues. Today, as he approaches age fifty, he's a political science professor at the University of Alberta in Edmonton focusing on international relations. He also coedits the quarterly journal *Global Governance,* a leading academic forum for debating the globalization process.

Knight became a Bahá'í through his wife, Mitra, an Iranian-born Bahá'í, whom he met at Dalhousie University in Halifax. His attraction to the religion is about far more than romance, though. For Knight, the faith offers a "holistic" approach that resonates with his work in support of creating a global government for managing the rapid change he believes is in critical need of a controlling force that pays more than lip service to the moral perspective.

"It's the unified whole presented in a spiritual framework," Knight says of the Bahá'í faith. "It's a holistic sense that all religions are seen as part of the same stream. It's holistic in seeing no split between science and religion; it's holistic in its view of all humanity as one. It's compatible with the ideas I have about multilateral institutions. Being a Bahá'í gives deeper meaning to what I attempt to do professionally because it places my ideas in a theological framework supported by the writings of the Messengers."

Knight calls himself a global citizen. So does Rebequa Getahoun Murphy, the daughter of an Ethiopian diplomat. Her upbringing, she says, "seems to have destined me to becoming a Bahá'í." She became one after leaving her native land for the University of Alaska and becoming friends with classmates who her own Ethiopian Coptic Church said were destined for hell because of their non-Christian beliefs. That clashed with the universalist in her, and she decided that Bahá'ís were right about the unity of religious thought. Today, she lives in Philadelphia and travels frequently as a management and job placement consultant. She's also the cofounder of the African Institute on Leadership and Government, an NGO that does leadership training, mostly for women, in Ethiopia.

Murphy—a member of the Bahá'í Board of Continental Counselors, an appointed body that assists elected Bahá'í officials throughout the Western Hemisphere (other regions have their own counselors)—says her talks to non-Bahá'ís are laced with references to transnational markets and other aspects of globalism in an effort to familiarize her listeners with the process as Bahá'ís understand it. Most people, she says, are simply bewildered by what's going on. "I often lecture on the evolution of the workplace from an agricultural focus to the postindustrial phase we are now in. People don't understand that they are part of an evolutionary process. Often they say to me, 'Wow, this is the first time someone has explained globalization to me in a way I can understand,'" she says.

Critics of globalization focus above all on the concentration of wealth and power that the process has shifted to corporations and international agencies whose sole concern, say the detractors, seems to be the unrestricted movement of goods and capital—and the bottom line. These critics say the market values that globalism advances have widened the gap between a rich elite and an impoverished world underclass. Globalism, they maintain, is no more than a new form of economic imperialism. However, Bahá'í leaders tend to support the facilitation of trade and financial transactions across national borders. For Bahá'ís, the process is in line with the global unification they hold so dear. One official statement reads:

> The period following World War II brought the establishment of institutions whose field of operation is global: the International Monetary Fund, the World Bank, the General Agreement on Tariffs and Trade, and a network of development agencies devoted to rationalizing and advancing the material prosperity of the planet. At century's end—whatever the intentions and however crude the present generation of tools—the masses of humanity have been shown that the use of the planet's wealth can be fundamentally reorganized in response to entirely new conceptions of need.[8]

Yet for all their optimism over globalization, Bahá'ís say they are by no means naive about the process. "The one challenge that we have as Bahá'ís is that sometimes we do appear almost Pollyannaish, but we are not," says Murphy. "In this process we try and go back and see how people lived in the past. When we lived in clans we could never imagine living in tribes, and those who advocated living in tribes were threatening. And when we lived in tribes we could not imagine living as a nation.... So now we come

along and say we should live as one global village, and that
sounds very threatening. We are at the very beginning stage
of globalization so there are lots of imbalances.... There are
very many things that do not make sense about the current
system, but the solution isn't to go back but to create a just
and fair system for everybody."

As with everything, Bahá'ís seek guidance on this
issue in the writing of Bahá'u'lláh, who cautioned that
globalization in its highest form would not come about
without "convulsions and chaos."[9] He likened the process
to the demolition of one building to make way for another.
It follows then that for Bahá'ís, the central question is how
to best insure that constructing the new economic order
entails as little harm as possible for people forced to adapt
to the accelerated change.

"Globalization is a two-edged sword," says Knight, the
professor in Canada. "The negative element is the dominant
liberal culture being imposed on people across the globe who
are not ready for it and are taken advantage of by it, which is
causing the backlash. Despite the promise, globalization has
brought about an even greater disparity.... Trickle down is
not working. There's an insensitivity to those on the margins
who are already poor and just getting poorer."

The Bahá'í response to this concern is the faith's concept of justice, conceived as

> the one power that can translate the dawning con-
> sciousness of humanity's oneness into a collective
> will through which the necessary structures of global
> community life can be confidently erected.... At the
> individual level, justice is that faculty of the human

soul that enables each person to distinguish truth from falsehood.... It calls for fair-mindedness in one's judgments, for equity in one's treatment of others, and is thus a constant if demanding companion in the daily occasions of life. At a group level, a concern for justice is the indispensable compass in collective decision making, because it is the only means by which unity of thought and action can be achieved. Far from encouraging the punitive spirit that has often masqueraded under its name in past ages, justice is the practical expression of awareness that, in the achievement of human progress, the interests of the individual and those of society are inextricably linked.[10]

Bahá'í optimism rests in the belief that justice, once determined through the faith's grassroots consultative process, ultimately prevails. Justice, say Bahá'ís, offsets "the temptation to sacrifice the well-being of the generality of humankind—and even the planet itself—to the advantages which technological breakthroughs can make available to privileged minorities."[11]

Justice must be the guiding concern in economic decisions if populations are to see the decisions as beneficial and fair, and be willing to carry them out, say Bahá'ís. Human rights lie at the heart of justice; every individual regardless of gender, class, race, or nationality must be educated and nurtured so that their potential can be reached, the caveat being that human rights must not be confused with "the cult of individualism that so deeply corrupts many areas of contemporary life."[12]

Said Bahá'u'lláh, "The light of men is Justice. Quench it not with the contrary winds of oppression and tyranny. The purpose of justice is the appearance of unity among men. The ocean of divine wisdom surgeth within this exalted word, while the books of the world cannot contain its inner significance."[13]

Faith in the essential goodness of all people. Faith in the persuasive power of reason. Faith in a unity within seemingly endless human diversity. That is Bahá'u'lláh's message of hope. For Bahá'ís, it's just a matter of time before it all comes to pass.

7

Tribal and Earth-Based Religions:
IN DEFENSE OF THE MOTHER

A LIGHT RAIN FALLS AS SEYDINA SENGHOR darts between the taxis and trucks that clog the midtown Manhattan street. A dashing figure in a bowler hat and dark blue pin-striped suit, an unopened black umbrella dangling from his left arm, he looks every bit the proper product of European colonialism that he is—except for the cowrie shells woven into his dreadlocks that hint at his Senegalese roots. A few minutes later, sitting in a tony hotel lobby frequented by the legal set, Senghor sips orange juice and pronounces himself to be pro-globalization—sort of.

"How could I be anything else? Look at who I am!" exclaims a smiling Senghor, who works as a part-time legal assistant in New York to fund his passions, which are working for Third World debt relief and running an organization he started to aid the city's African immigrants. "But my idea of globalization is a globalization of justice, of solidarity between people. We're for globalizing hope. Economic globalization is not what I mean. That's not doing much for my people at this point."

The next afternoon, the Synod House at the Cathedral Church of St. John the Divine—the Upper West Side Manhattan landmark that calls itself the world's largest cathedral—is packed with several hundred people on hand for a rally. Most appear no older than their mid-twenties, and all of them are strongly opposed to corporate globalization and what they consider to be its unmitigated evils. Backpacks and facial piercings are the favored accessories. Protest signs expressing utter disdain for capitalism and solidarity with a myriad of environmental and minority causes proliferate. Starhawk, arguably the twenty-first century's best-known "Witch," her preferred spiritual self-identity, is the first speaker.

"The viability of the planet has to be our highest priority. It can't be second to profits. Putting profits first is not only evil, it's stupid," says Starhawk, a practitioner of the "Old Religion" reformulation known as Wicca, a Goddess-based, holistic, and environmentally oriented neo-pagan movement experiencing rapid growth and a spate of public attention. "The promise of corporate capitalism is that the economy is infinite and ever expanding. But no tide rises forever without becoming a complete catastrophe."

Senghor's spiritual roots are a mix of Islamic and Christian influences superimposed on the traditional beliefs of his tribal group, Senegal's Serer people. Starhawk, born an American of Jewish heritage, has adopted a belief system that is a modern reclaiming of Europe's own mostly forgotten, pre-Christian tribal spirituality.

Where they come together is in the deep connection that indigenous tribal and contemporary Earth-based traditions maintain to the forces that animate the natural world—a cosmology that the monotheistic faiths shifted heavenward as they constructed dualistic notions of divinity running counter to the undifferentiated sacredness of their spiritual antecedents. It is within this worldview that the innate suspicions of globalization shared by Senghor and Starhawk originate.

That is not to say that tribal beliefs and neo-paganism are synonymous, however. The opposite is very much the case. True, both descend from memory. But the former constitute unbroken memories tied to specific peoples and equally specific geography (witness the North American Plains tribes' spiritual identification with the bison, in contrast to the Northwest tribes' identification with the salmon), while the latter comprises contemporary creations drawn from memories of an often idealized religious past whose appeal is in large part its rejection of today's generic, Western, urbanized culture that neo-pagans find wanting.

"Neo-pagans are trying to construct a system similar to what we call tribal. They are appropriating tribal values as a critique of their own culture. But I question the degree to which they can really escape their own culture," says Ifi Amadiume, who teaches courses on indigenous African religion at Dartmouth College. Starhawk concurs. "Most tribal people grow up immersed in a worldview that supports [their] beliefs, whereas most...neo-pagans are finding our way back to them out of a culture which denies or denigrates them," she says. Neo-pagans, she cautions, run the risk of being trivial when they naively believe they can slip into a new paradigm simply by engaging in Native American, African, or rituals of their own creation.

Huston Smith, the eminent scholar of comparative religion, refers to tribal tradition as "primal" religiosity "because it came first." He notes the big five "historical" religions—Buddhism, Hinduism, Judaism, Christianity, and Islam—that now claim most of the world's population "form only the tip of the religious iceberg, for they span a scant four thousand years as compared with the three million years or so of the religions that preceded them.... This mode of religion continues in Africa, Australia, Southeast Asia, the Pacific Islands, Siberia, and among the Indians of North and South America."[1]

"Holistic" has become a much-overused word, but it remains appropriate when talking about tribal spirituality, even though indigenous beliefs vary widely in their particulars no less than Christianity's seemingly endless profusion of sects and subsects. *Holistic* applies to tribal spirituality because life is perceived as an interconnected

> Indigenous tribal and contemporary Earth-based traditions each maintain a deep connection to the forces that animate the natural world, but the traditions are not synonymous. Tribal beliefs constitute unbroken memory tied to specific peoples and equally specific geography, while neo-pagans are contemporary creations drawn from memories of an often idealized religious past whose appeal is in large part its rejection of today's generic, Western, urbanized culture.

whole. But it also applies because of the way "religion" itself is conceptualized by tribal groups. Bucknell University professor of religion John A. Grim explains it as follows:

> Central to indigenous traditions is an awareness of the integral and whole relationship of symbolic and material life. Ritual practices and the cosmological ideas which undergird society cannot be separated out as an institutionalized religion from the daily round of subsistence practices.... To analyze religion as a separate system of beliefs and ritual practices apart from subsistence, kinship, language, governance, and landscape is to misunderstand indigenous religion.[2]

In a nutshell, religion in the tribal consciousness is nothing less than the warp and woof of life itself.

But centuries of colonization and now globalization have left uncontaminated tribal beliefs teetering on the edge of extinction. Senghor's one million Serer co-tribalists have become the norm: outwardly, most profess membership in the club of historical religions; inwardly, most retain at least some of their traditional belief in the forces of creation. "Pre-colonial Africa survives with its institutions and beliefs running parallel to the Western institutions imposed on us," explains Senghor, the nephew of Senegal's first president and renowned poet, Léopold Sédar Senghor. Nigeria's Igbo people, Amadiume's tribal group, have undergone a similar transformation. "Since colonialization, the Igbo have been converted to Christianity, mostly

Anglican and Roman Catholic, but now [to] neo-Christian sects as well that are more matriarchal and involved with healing like the traditional beliefs," she says. "But even those who go to church go home and evoke their ancestors."

Nor are tribal people confined to their homelands anymore. Today's ease of global travel makes it possible to find modern tribal people walking the streets of Western capitals, where they test the waters of the globalized economy and work the established channels for dissent when the same globalized economy threatens their homeland. The U'wa, a tribe of just five thousand people from northwest Colombia, for example, sent a delegation to Washington, D.C., in the spring of 2002 to lobby for the preservation of their Andean rain forest homeland, which worldwide oil giant Occidental Petroleum wants for exploration and extraction. Asked whether he found Washington interesting, U'wa spokesman Armando Tegria Vincunada responded, "A real interesting thing for me is an untouched forest."[3]

Taking it a step further, the nomadic Masai people of Kenya and Tanzania—legendary for their warrior past and known by their red tunics and traditional dances featuring high leaps—maintain a branch of the tribe's legal defense fund in Washington year-round. Meitamel Olol-Dapash is the full-time Masai representative in the U.S. capital. His efforts focus on opposing schemes by the Kenyan and Tanzanian governments—working with multinational and domestic corporations—to take over Masai land for development. Much of his time is spent lobbying international agencies such as the World Bank in an attempt to make their East Africa projects less harmful to the Masai.

To be sure, some of the Masai opposition is rooted in political and economic self-interests that are no different than those of Western elites. But as with the U'wa, the Masai articulate their opposition to the exploitation of their ancestral land by outsiders in language reflecting the indigenous worldview explained by Grim. Call it eco-sacred.

The pastoral Masai have already lost more than 75 percent of what was their traditional homeland. Now, the Mau forest, the Masai "promised land," is threatened. The 412,000-acre region just north of the Tanzania-Kenya border, says Olol-Dapash, "is not just the foundation of our livelihood but it is also the foundation of our spirituality. Land is central to our spiritual beliefs because we believe that God dwells not only in and beyond the deep-blue skies...but also in the thick forests, rivers, and beneath the earth." The Mau forest is particularly important to the Masai because as their "promised land" it is the place that holds "our future, our prosperity, the resources for our cultural reproduction and the cohesiveness of our society," says Olol-Dapash.[4]

Many of the roughly four hundred thousand remaining Masai have nominally converted to the Christianity of their erstwhile British rulers. But they still retreat to the Mau forest for initiation ceremonies, periods of spiritual renewal, and to collect healing plants that are seen as curing both physical illness and spiritual malaise. British colonialism cost the Masai dearly. Now, Olol-Dapash says, globalization threatens what remains of their culture's spiritual and social underpinning.

"Globalization is bad in a big way. It's sweeping in like a big wave. We play no role in the designing of any programs that will intensify the pressures we already feel. Our indigenous spiritual values can be of significant benefit to globalization, but it is difficult to get the powerful people to hear that. Conservation of natural resources could be very beneficial to international tourism. Our way of life is livestock based. If it's not destroyed it can benefit the national economy. Allow the forest to remain and it can advance pharmacology by drawing on the healing plants," he says.

> Concern for the land—an innate environmental ethic—is a prime cause of indigenous suspicions toward globalization. A second major cause is the social and economic values that globalization embodies. Tribal people tend to conceptualize family and property differently from Westerners, for whom the extended family is being reduced to a list of Internet addresses, for whom community may mean this year's social grouping, and for whom home is a financial investment whose value reflects the market rather than deep roots.

Concern for the land—an innate environmental ethic—is a prime cause of indigenous suspicions toward globalization. A second major cause is the social and economic values that globalization embodies. Tribal people tend to conceptualize family and property differently from Westerners, for whom the extended family is being reduced to a list of Internet addresses, for whom community may mean this year's social grouping, and for whom home is a financial investment whose value reflects the market rather than deep roots. Take the Igbo, for example.

The Igbo, a thirty-million-strong linguistic group, traditionally expressed "matriarchal social values" that Amadiume says produced an agricultural society in which power was decentralized, land was never a commodity, and social connections were cemented by a belief that all Igbo were "children of one mother [the goddess Idemili] who ate out of one pot [and were] bound by the spirit of common motherhood." Patriarchal values associated with competition and warfare were also evidenced, of course, but were mitigated by "the Earth goddess," considered the "most important deity, guardian of morality, and controller of the economy." Sharing was in and greed was out. Capitalism was unknown; monetary exchanges did not exist.[5]

The Igbo system began to break down under the slave trade, a sort of proto-globalization that ran its course from the fifteenth through the nineteenth centuries. The colonialism that followed, says Amadiume, further "forced" greed on the Igbo through the imposition of taxes, which in turn led to the necessity of planting cash crops, labor migration, and the sale of land. As bad as colonialism was, though, Amadiume saves her harshest criticism for contemporary globalization's impact on the Igbo, and on much of Africa. Her charge is that the "neo-liberal global economic order" merely perpetuates colonialism while it further "alienates African people from their indigenous ways and wisdom," as well as encouraging the utter subjugation of women by giving full rein to imported and indigenous patriarchal values that denigrate less valued matriarchal codes of conduct. She fumes:

Post-colonial Eurocentric development ideals introduced the separation between religion, economics, and social life with principles that support human domination over nature and the separation of humans from other living things. African traditional religious thought would see the global economic principles that are operational today as emanating from the mechanical world view of those without totem, those without taboos or ritual restrictions. Traditional Africans believe that the spiritual upheavals in Africa today emanate from the entry of bad spirits; these bad spirits pollute the environment, pollute the mind, and waste lives. Local beliefs articulate the many faces of the economy of globalization, class exploitation, poverty, and social afflictions.[6]

Starhawk also fumes at globalization but, devoid of tribal connections to a specific geography, she and other neo-pagans speak in more general environmental terms, although they also invoke matriarchal spiritual images and longing for a sharing community. It should be noted, however, that while all neo-pagan groups share some characteristics, such as Earth-based god and goddess worship and ritual celebrations anchored in the solstices and other seasonal passages, they also constitute a diverse movement. Not all reflect Starhawk's radical left-wing political orientation or activist bent. By way of contrast, Ásatrú, another modern neo-pagan movement that draws on the ancient Norse and Germanic gods and goddesses, has proven attractive to some right-wing and libertarian neo-pagans.

Starhawk came by her name (she was born Miriam Simos) through a dream, experienced during a particularly hard time in her life. In the dream, she recounts, a hawk "swooped down and turned into an old woman. I felt that I was under her protection." An itinerant tarot card and palm reader at the time, she combined the hawk with the tarot deck's Star card, "which represents the Deep Self," to come up with a new name and a new identity as a Wiccan.[7]

Wicca is the largest of the growing number of Earth-based religious groups, but even within the Wiccan stream there are several currents drawing on Celtic, Druidic, Greek, Roman, Egyptian, and other ancient paths. Margot Adler, best known as a National Public Radio correspondent, but also a public Wiccan for more than a quarter-century, says Wicca's "great strength" is its flexibility that "exists because Wicca is not wedded to one truth. But to be honest, there have always been many versions of Wicca, and not all of them have celebrated or felt comfortable with diversity and freedom."[8]

Starhawk, in her groundbreaking work *The Spiral Dance: A Rebirth of the Ancient Religion of the Great Goddess,* first published in 1979 and a best-seller credited with heightening the movement's profile immeasurably, says the term *Wicca* comes from the Anglo-Saxon word meaning "to bend or shape."[9] Wiccans, she explains, are a contemporary, feminist reconstitution of the fertility sects that were among the earliest attempts at human understanding of life and, perhaps more important, death— Smith's "primal religion." Wiccan tradition teaches that the Old Religion was driven underground, and eventually into near oblivion, by patriarchal and Christian persecution, which equated the preexisting feminine spirituality with the Devil.

To be a Witch, a word Starhawk admits is confusing if not scary to the uninitiated, and which Wiccans capitalize to honor and set it apart from the stereotype, is to engage in "the Craft," the altering of normal reality evoked by Wicca etymology. Witchcraft corresponds to the traditional shamanism (a word derived from Siberian tribal culture) of indigenous groups that is characterized by ritually evoking an alternative or heightened state of consciousness for the purpose of communing with the spirit world, often with the intent of healing. The Craft, it follows, is a form of religious ecstasy, and to be a Witch is to be a religious initiate.

Wiccans are said by various estimates to number as many as two hundred thousand or more in the United States, with similar numbers estimated for Britain and elsewhere in the Western world. However, precise numbers are impossible to come by because of the diversity and independence of Wiccan groups, and because many practitioners remain solitary or prefer to keep their identities secret, out of fear they will be looked upon askance or even face overt persecution, notes John M. Morris, editor of *Seeker Journal*, a neo-pagan monthly magazine published in Ann Arbor, Michigan.

"I'd say 80 percent of Wiccans and other neo-pagans are on their own and are probably more active in connecting with each other on the Internet than any other way," says Morris, a retired philosophy professor and Unitarian Universalist minister who also calls himself a Witch (yes, men may be Witches; in fact a retired British civil servant named Gerald B. Gardner is generally credited with formulating Wiccan concepts in the 1930s, although women predominate in the movement today).

Morris's noting of the Internet's importance to neo-pagans is both telling and ironic, and undoubtedly true. At Beliefnet.com, a multi-faith Web magazine for which I served as news director, Wiccans and other neo-pagans were among the most engaged of all readers, aggressively demanding equal time for their holidays and views and posting voluminous opinions. (The Web site Witches' Voice, founded in 1995—which makes it a certified pioneer as far as the Internet goes—was the 2002 spirituality category's People's Choice Webbie winner, the digital media equivalent of the Oscars. Ironically, Beliefnet finished second.) The global communications network that has also allowed transnational corporations to do their will has enabled neo-pagans to escape their isolation and gain a forum while maintaining anonymity. "The Internet supplied the safe meeting ground Pagans and Witches had not had for centuries," says Starhawk, who, like Adler, was a popular Beliefnet columnist.[10]

Wiccans and other neo-pagans preach immanence, interconnection, and community; the divine is present in the natural world, all life is interdependent, and sharing creates compassion and harmony. "Love for life in all its forms is the basic ethic of Witchcraft.... Serving the life force means working to preserve the diversity of the natural life, to prevent the poisoning of the environment and the destruction of the species," says Starhawk, whose globetrotting schedule takes her from street protests at World Bank meetings, to leading workshops on sustainable growth and permaculture, to training "global justice" activists, and more at a breakneck pace.[11] She does it, she maintains, because the three patriarchal Abrahamic faiths, in particular, have failed to serve the life force by virtue of their having separated God from nature, thereby placing the environment outside the parameters of the divine and paving the way—literally, at times—for its mindless exploitation and destruction.

> Wiccans and other neo-pagans preach immanence, interconnection, and community; God or Goddess is present in the natural world, all life is interdependent, and sharing creates compassion and harmony. They believe the three patriarchal Abrahamic faiths, in particular, have failed to serve the "life force" by virtue of their having separated God from nature, thereby placing the environment outside the parameters of the divine and paving the way—literally, at times—for its mindless exploitation and destruction.

That all sounds familiar to Seydina Senghor. "The attitude of the West, which is the attitude of globalization, is aggressiveness toward nature," he says, the colonial legacy of a French accent discernible in his voice.

> For Africans, nature is God and God is nature. God in *her* plurality has multiple ways of replicating *herself* and you can see it in the animal form.... [The Serer] believe that when you meet someone you should leave them in better shape than when you came. That's a central Serer value. Globalization is not doing that.... We say that if you cannot give it, don't take it. Don't take from people what you cannot give

them. You cannot give life, only Creation can do that, so don't take it from anyone. This is what Western structures do. This is what international debt does....
We have an imbalance.

In *The Way of the Animal Powers, Volume 1,* the famed mythologist Joseph Campbell notes that Siberian shamans—"whose spirits are believed to fly"—wear bird costumes.[12] Today, neo-pagans incorporate the names of birds into their own names. The connection is obvious. Tribal people fight globalization's negative encroachment because they sense its accompanying spiritual disenfranchisement, even as they employ the advancements of globalization in the process. Neo-pagan criticism springs forth from the experience of advanced disenfranchisement, even as they, too, pick and choose what they like from globalism's complex menu. Perhaps that's evidence enough of life's essential nature. Call it holistic.

8

Protestantism:
GOING BY THE BOOK

IN THE EARLY NINETEENTH CENTURY, when Harlem was still a rural community known as Manhattanville, Saint Mary's Episcopal Church took a bold step: in deference to the parish's poorer members it abandoned the then-common practice of requiring worshippers to pay a rental fee to sit in its pews. Two centuries later, Saint Mary's remains a church committed to its poorer congregants. Only now, the parish sees their poverty in a global context.

Saint Mary's spiritual leader is the Reverend Earl Kooperkamp, a high-energy white Southerner guiding a mostly African-American congregation on the western edge of America's most famous black community. Saint Mary's, he says, is "on the liberal end" of the Episcopal spectrum "and proud of it," which is to say that the 175-member parish—a redbrick remnant of Protestant mainline aristocracy in a sea of upstart storefront churches—eagerly participates in a myriad of social causes. Crime, violence, justice, peace, racism, police brutality, poverty, low wages; organize a demonstration or a project and count on the participation of Saint Mary's.

Characteristically, Kooperkamp and a small contingent from Saint Mary's joined the street protests that condemned transnational corporate policies when the World Economic Forum brought leading proponents and opponents of the globalization movement to New York in early 2002. "We in the church tend to spiritualize power, like talking about the power of the Holy Spirit. But globalization is often about down and dirty politics, and that means going downtown and protesting when the opportunity presents itself," says Kooperkamp.

Yet for all his clarity of purpose, Kooperkamp is acutely aware of what he regards as his church's built-in contradiction. "I believe globalization is a positively wrong headed way to live together on this earth," says Kooperkamp, who is in his mid-forties. "It is just leading to further and further inequality between people, and further and further environmental degradation." At the same time, he adds, "the Anglican Communion [of which the Episcopal Church is the American branch] is an institution of globalization. That is its power and that is its weakness as well, because as an institution of globalization the church is part of a power structure that is exploitative. British colonialism is what spread the church and brought it worldwide wealth and adherents. But to achieve this the Anglican Church had to look the other way at certain practices of the ruling class. The consequences of this haunt us to this day."

Kooperkamp's comments touch on a profound question for Christians: What is the church's role in a world increasingly dominated by a hyper-secular market economy dismissive and undermining of religious traditions? The question yields no easy answer, of course, giving rise instead to a host of competing responses. Perhaps nowhere are the answers more divergent than among the world's more than 400 million Protestant Christians, an appropriate placement given their legacy as heirs to a spiritual rebellion that placed its faith in individual religious expression. The response to globalization has only heightened the differences.

An explanation of the term *Christian* is in order before we proceed. "Christian" is often used by conservative Protestants to differentiate themselves (and by doing so to stake a claim of authenticity) from members of Roman Catholic, Orthodox, liberal Protestant, and other churches that regard themselves, and are regarded by others, as being equally Christian—that is, derived from the teachings of Jesus of Nazareth. My use of the term is meant here to be both inclusive and exclusive, depending upon the context.

Why explain this? Because Christians are a disparate lot who differ greatly over Jesus' nature and the intent of his message, and have done so ever since the religion's early days when church councils ruled on the orthodoxy of various positions, creating divisions that often turned bloody and which persist to this day.

Was Jesus the Son of God, the promised Messiah—the Christ (from the Greek *Christos*)—promised in the Hebrew Scripture known to Christians as the Old Testament? That's the view of traditionalists. Or was he a mortal man, a first-century Jewish prophet who articulated the pain and spirit of his people and was crucified for doing so by the Roman overlords of first-century Judea? Some liberal Christians say this statement is more historically accurate. Either way, Jesus' "preaching about the kingdom of God held political implications by announcing an alternative order of divine rule. In the end, Jesus was executed by the Romans, crucified as a traitor to the Roman state," notes David Chidester, author of *Christianity: A Global History*.[1]

Jesus' death, of course, did not end his ministry. His teachings—and Christians who interpret the Resurrection literally would say Jesus himself—live on, and what began as a persecuted sect went from underdog to top dog with the conversion to Christianity three centuries later of the Roman emperor Constantine. The church's relationship to worldly power has been clouded ever since.

The Protestant domain—splintered as it is by beliefs, practices, and ethnicity into thousands of church groups and subgroups—reflects this ambiguity, perhaps even more so than do Christendom's other main branches, the more hierarchical Roman Catholic and Orthodox churches. For just as Protestant Anglicans aligned themselves with the state, Protestant Anabaptists—Mennonites, Amish, and others who adhere to pacifism and strict church-state separation—set themselves apart from secular power even when it meant persecution by their coreligionists. Today, globalized commerce, communications, and culture have further complicated the Protestant response. Hence, any attempt to explain the Protestant reaction to globalization by resorting alone to such theological categorizations as "liberal" and "conservative" falls far short of conveying this enormous complexity.

Take the Episcopal Church, for example. Just as Kooperkamp stands to the left in his denomination's "social gospel" wing, Tom Sine's self-definition as an "evangelical Episcopalian" might ordinarily pigeonhole him as a member of his church's right wing. Yet Sine, a Seattle-based "futures consultant" to mission-oriented Christian organizations, is also highly critical of globalization's negative consequences, including many of those articulated by Kooperkamp. Sine is most critical of what he terms globalization's "values impact."

"I don't think the global economic order is just about global commerce," says Sine, author of *Mustard Seed versus McWorld: Reinventing Life and Faith for the Future*.

> I think it's having a huge values impact that is generally overlooked by most evangelicals who are far too enchanted with the free market to notice. But in Christianity, the "Ultimate" is never defined principally in economic terms, and that's just what globalization does. For Christians, the Ultimate is spiritual and societal transformation, the celebration of life and relationships. That's very different than the economic emphasis of globalization. The values of globalization stand in fundamental opposition to the values of the Gospel.[2]

Protestant churches were born of the sixteenth-century Reformation, the Western Christian movement that rejected the Roman papacy and, more important to our context, gave primacy to biblical authority. Protestants may differ over inerrancy, emphasis, and meaning, but they share broad agreement that the Bible, comprising both the Old and New Testaments, is *a* if not *the* source of eternal spiritual truth. It therefore behooves us to consider relevant biblical concepts to understand Protestant perspectives on globalization.

Let's begin by looking at the belief that everything on earth, and by extension globalization as well, is part of the unfolding progression of God's own plan "to be put into effect when the times will have reached their fulfillment— to bring all things in heaven and earth together under one head, even Christ" (Ephesians 1:10).

"Globalization should not surprise Christians, who confess that God created one world and sent forth the first man and woman to populate," says James W. Skillen, president of the evangelical-oriented Center for Public Justice in Annapolis, Maryland.

For Skillen, globalization is no less a part of God's creation than were the biblical Adam and Eve. And because Adam and Eve's "first disobedience" has been followed by "multigenerational disobedience to the Creator, who entrusted us with so much," Christians also should not be surprised by the myriad problems Skillen blames on human mishandling of globalization's challenge.[3]

No matter how formidable and seemingly corruptive those problems may appear, adds Bob Goudzwaard, a Dutch evangelical professor, politician, and antipoverty advocate, because the entirety of creation is of God,

Christians still must honor "the intrinsic goodness" contained within the process of globalization, as with all aspects of the "fallen" world in which they live. "However critical we may be of human irresponsibility and disobedience...we must never become doomsayers about technology as such, or about governments as such, or about markets as such. We may not demonize what God has given us."[4]

Goudzwaard counsels a contextual and evenhanded consideration of globalization, with a special emphasis on

---

Biblical principles gird core Protestant attitudes toward globalization. Chief among them are:

- Globalization as part of God's plan "to be put into effect when the times will have reached their fulfillment—to bring all things in heaven and earth together under one head, even Christ" (Ephesians 1:10)
- The Great Commission: Jesus' exhortation to "make disciples of all the nations, baptizing them in the name of the Father and of the Son and of the Holy Spirit" (Matthew 28:19)
- Stewardship: the belief that the spirit of God is in all of creation—*His* creation—and that humans are required to use wisely that which they have been blessed to receive. "Heaven is my throne, and the earth is my footstool.... Has not my hand made all these things?" (Acts 7:49–50)
- The demand for justice and ethical living: expressed by the prophet Isaiah as "seek justice, encourage the oppressed, defend the fatherless, plead the case of the widow" (Isaiah 1:17), and by Paul in admonishing Rome's earliest Christians to "share with God's people who are in need" and "do what is right in the eyes of everybody" (Romans 12:13, 17)

working to mitigate its destructive economic, environmental, and social ramifications. David E. Bay also subscribes to the belief that globalization and the entirety of creation is of God and God's plan. But beyond that shared core belief, Bay and Goudzwaard agree on little else concerning globalization—or God's plan.

Working from the basement of his home in the southeast Massachusetts community of Attleboro, Bay directs Cutting Edge Ministries, which has as its logo a gold cross and a sword dripping blood. Bay describes his organization as "a fundamental, independent Baptist Church outreach ministry" that seeks to "forewarn God's people" about the "New World Order" that will result, inevitably, in the "soon appearance of the Antichrist" in accordance with "His prophecies and Biblical doctrines."

In sum, Cutting Edge Ministries regards globalization as nothing less than a sign of the imminent appearance of the Antichrist, whom theological literalists such as Bay consider a real figure who will lead the forces of evil at the final battle presaging Christ's victory and the establishment on Earth of the Kingdom of God.

Bay's worldview holds that the "satanic influences" that flourish in the form of the United Nations, the International Monetary Fund and World Bank, the Masons, New Age beliefs, the environmental movement, the social gospel movement, feminism, ecumenism, global communications networks, the spread of Islam, consumerism, religious pluralism, "liberalism," and more, will gain global control for the exceedingly horrific, seven-year period known as "the Tribulation," which will end with the victorious return to earth of Jesus Christ. It's all been ordained by "the one, true" God, says Bay, and there simply is no way around it.

For Bay, then, globalization is the process by which unimaginable evil will be unleashed in the form of a new world war, the persecution of "God's people," and widespread death and destruction on an unprecedented scale—all of it God's plan for the end of worldly history. It's all pretty grim, and yet you would be wrong to assume that Bay does not welcome globalization. Flippantly put, Bay believes that without the pain there can be no gain, which in this case is the establishment of the Kingdom of God.

Some fundamentalist Protestants regard globalization as nothing less than a sign of the imminent appearance of the Antichrist, whom theological literalists consider a real figure who will lead the forces of evil at the final battle presaging Christ's victory and the establishment on earth of the Kingdom of God. Says David Bay, director of Cutting Edge Ministries, "We are glad to see that our position is being upheld, that God is forcing the demonic host to fulfill his prophecy. It's an exciting time to be alive, because once again, and for the final time, you can see the prophecy fulfilled in the daily news and the Bible is proven true."

"We are glad to see that our position is being upheld, that God is forcing the demonic host to fulfill his prophecy. It's an exciting time to be alive, because once again, and for the final time, you can see the prophecy fulfilled in the daily news and the Bible is proven true," he says.

You would also be wrong to assume that Bay's beliefs

are so radical that they would relegate him to some thinly populated Protestant fringe. Forget the clichéd mental picture of an unpainted, backwoods church where he and a like-minded remnant worship in inbred isolation. The reality is far from that.

One proof is the phenomenal success of the *Left Behind* novels, the all-time best-selling Christian fiction series with sales so far of more than fifty million copies in twenty-one languages. The series, cowritten by Tim LaHaye and Jerry Jensen, both of whom describe themselves as evangelicals, is based on an interpretation of Bible theology found, in the main, in the apocalyptic Book of Revelation, the last book of the New Testament, that conservative interpreters consider a literal telling, or prophecy, of the persecution and final triumph of the faithful preceding Jesus' Second Coming.

LaHaye and Jensen prefer literary craftsmanship to Bay's sledgehammer rhetoric to make their point. But aside from style and tone they differ little from Bay's conclusions about globalization and religious truth.

Moreover, surveys commissioned by the publisher of the *Left Behind* series conclude that large numbers of American Protestants subscribe to the beliefs upon which the novels are based, and that some 45 percent of the series' readers classify themselves as members of the educated, suburban, baby-boomer generation. So instead of frenzied holy rollers, picture soccer moms contemplating the apocalyptic. Presumably, they share belief in some of what LaHaye and Jensen present as the truth about globalization. At the very least, their reading pushes them toward considering the possibility.

Tom Sine, for one, finds that prospect alarming because of what he says is *Left Behind*'s fatalistic message that working for social change is useless, since God has already dictated that "everything is determined to get worse and worse," and that "the best we can do is to get a few more people in the salvation boat before Jesus comes back."[5]

Whether *Left Behind* readers also feel a sense of irony over contributing to a publishing phenomenon that is itself made possible by the globalized economic and communications systems now in place is unknown. Bay acknowledges that sense of irony in his own effort, even if it enjoys considerably less commercial success.

Cutting Edge Ministries began life as an outreach mission of a flesh-and-blood congregation. But today it exists solely on the Internet. Bay says his Web ministry is accessed 200,000 to 300,000 times each month by computer users in ninety nations, who keep his ministry economically afloat by subscribing to his Web site and purchasing books, tapes, CDs, and articles offered for sale. No globalized economic and communications networks, no Cutting Edge Ministries, admits Bay.

"Up until the point where the Antichrist takes over, there is no problem taking part in global activity," he says. "Obviously, one should participate as a Christian and not compromise that principle, and there are ways in which it is more difficult to participate than other ways. If you're in banking it's a lot harder than being a small businessman. But for every person, there will come a time when they can no longer participate."

For Bible-believing Protestants, a second important consideration regarding globalization is the exhortation from Jesus to spread God's word, to "make disciples of all the nations, baptizing them in the name of the Father and of the Son and of the Holy Spirit" (Matthew 28:19). Seen from this vantage point, globalization is an efficient way to further "the Great Commission"—the spread of Christian thought and culture through proselytism. There are said to be about two billion Christians in the world and some 700 million of them are estimated to believe that advancing the Great Commission is central to their faith.[6]

Sine, despite his broad criticism of the process, also sees value in the helping hand that globalization has provided the spread of Western beliefs and institutions rooted in the Protestant ethic. He says:

Not only is the globalization of communications dramatically changing the ways in which we relate to one another, but it is also decisively changing how we conduct politics. One of the immediate benefits of using the [Inter]net to create a global economic order is that world leaders have been motivated to work for political stability, because conflict and war are expensive and get in the way of doing business. The architects of McWorld are a major force, therefore, for peace and stability in our world.[7]

Paul, the Apostle to the Gentiles, was the first to turn Jesus' injunction into action by taking the gospel message to the non-Jewish communities of Asia Minor and

Mediterranean Europe. Thus freed from the restraints of
Mosaic Law, the fledgling Jesus sect was set on its way to
becoming a world faith welcoming of all believers—the dictate to spread the faith to the earth's four corners was made
deed. One can look upon Paul's effort as the birth of the
global outlook, and globalization as the contemporary
equivalent, in essence, of the first-century Roman roads
that he traversed in his zeal to convert. Here's Goudzwaard
again:

> The Christian church—the body of Christ—was,
> from the start, also meant to become a global com-
> munity. While some of Jesus' disciples wanted to
> restrict the gospel message to the Jewish people,
> the Holy Spirit made it clear that all nations of the
> world should hear the Good News and participate
> in the new life. Thus, long before the present
> process of technological and economic globaliza-
> tion began, God's message of global good news
> went forth and began its work. The idea of global-
> ization, therefore, is not foreign to the Bible.[8]

Max L. Stackhouse, the eminent professor of
Christian ethics at Princeton University, also notes the
influence that Christianity, and in particular the faith's
Protestant form, has had on globalization's development.
The perception of those individuals in the developing world
who resist globalization as a foreign intrusion holds "a certain cogency," he says, because "it was in the West generally and in America particularly, deeply stamped by centuries
of Christianity, that developments fomenting contemporary

forms of capitalism, and, thus, globalization were nurtured."[9]

Others connect globalization and Protestantism more directly, but not necessarily more kindly. James Kurth, a political scientist and a conservative lay Presbyterian, calls globalization "Protestantism without God," a sort of twenty-first-century secular "American Creed" that has swept the world. Globalization's emphasis on individualism, its "contempt for and protest against all hierarchies, communities, traditions, and customs" is, says Kurth, the "ultimate extreme of the secularization of the Protestant religion" by the contemporary United States.[10]

From the Mediterranean, Christianity spread northward (setting aside, but not overlooking, important developments in Armenia and Ethiopia), where the faith was transformed to meet the cultural expectations of its newest adherents. "In art and popular thought, Jesus became a blond Aryan, often with the appropriate warrior attributes, and Christian theology was reshaped by West European notions of law and feudalism," says Pennsylvania State University's Philip Jenkins, author of *The Next Christendom: The Coming of Global Christianity*.[11] From there, Christianity was brought to the Americas, central and southern Africa, and East Asia by European explorers and traders accompanied by missionaries of various ilk: Catholic, Orthodox, and, of course, Protestant.

In the Americas, Catholics were the first to plant the cross, but Protestants soon followed with successes of their own, particularly in the northern regions that became Canada and the United States. Today, however, even largely Catholic South America is experiencing an explosion in

Protestant church membership resulting from an influx of evangelical and Pentecostal missionaries whose theology of personal salvation is attracting growing numbers of the formerly Catholic. In Asia and Africa as well, Protestant churches have been equally successful in carrying out the Great Commission. But by far the fastest growing segment of the Protestant world—and the Christian world in general—is the theologically (and often politically) conservative Pentecostal movement, which began in twentieth-century America. Pentecostals, who also fall within the broader evangelical definition, are known for their belief in the "gifts of the Holy Spirit"—including spiritual healing of physical ailments and speaking in tongues. The movement has become so popular that followers can even be found in Catholic and mainline Protestant congregations, where they are often called charismatics. The movement has embraced global communications—radio, television, and now the Internet—as an efficient means to expand its message and connect its far-flung adherents, even as its messengers rile against the immorality they see as permeating the secular media.

"According to current projections, the number of Pentecostal believers should surpass the one billion mark before 2050. In terms of global religions, there will be by that point as many Pentecostals as Hindus, and twice as many as there are Buddhists," says Jenkins, who identifies Pentecostalism "as perhaps the most successful social movement of the last century."[12]

Because Pentecostals emphasize individual salvation, and often profess what Jenkins refers to as a personal "health and wealth gospel," they are likely to be less hostile to economic and monoculture globalization than many other Christians. As Pentecostals continue to grow and gain influence in the developing world, over time that could mean a lessening of the intense opposition to globalization that exists today among Third World populations—who have benefited relatively little so far from the transnational market's laissez-faire policies. But should Third World Pentecostals fare no better in the future than their country-men, poverty and a sense of being wronged are likely to off-set whatever theological disposition they may have to Western ways perceived as inherently Christian.

The planting of Protestant forms that derive from North American and European church culture is one of Western Christianity's contributions to the developing world. (Whether one views this in a positive or negative light is another matter.) But globalization works both ways, and it may be said that the Southern hemisphere's return contribution has been to reinvigorate the North's atrophy-ing Protestant establishment, which in recent decades has been outdistanced by the growth of the evangelical and Pentecostal churches.

This contribution has come in the form of new immi-grant communities being established as globalization makes it easier to start life anew elsewhere. It's also appar-ent in the relatively recent practice of developing nations sending missionaries to the West, which has reversed cen-turies of church assumptions. Stirred as only the newly empowered can be, these missionaries bring to the task a fervor that many commentators say is rarely found anymore among Western Protestants, particularly in Europe, where the established churches are in the steepest decline. Centuries of global expansion combined with the twentieth-century West's creeping secularization and growing free-form spirituality detached from ancestral paths has turned Christianity into a largely non-Western religion.

Jehu Hanciles, a theologian from Sierra Leone based at the evangelical Fuller Theological Seminary in Pasadena, California, notes that there are now seven times as many Anglicans in Nigeria (once a British colony) as there are Episcopalians in the United States. Hanciles says that Christianity's—and particularly Pentecostalism's—rapid growth in Africa "raises the question of whether Africa needs American ministries as much as American ministries need Africa."[13]

The contemporary mission movement may be unprecedented in its ability to reach previously "unchurched" peoples, but it is by no means the first such evangelization effort. As stated, the church has always been about mission work. An example of how systematic the process can be is evident in the history of the Spanish-speaking states of Central America. In 1915, several dozen American Protestant church missionary groups meeting in Panama agreed to cooperate rather than compete for converts among the largely Catholic population by dividing up the region. El Salvador was given over to the denomination known today as American Baptist Churches in the U.S.A.

This division of mission field labor explains why Marta Benavides chose an American Baptist seminary when she decided she needed to become a minister to further her ecumenical work among the poor in her native El Salvador. Ordained though she may be, the Reverend Benavides has little patience for her church, and even less respect for its past record in her homeland. Benavides is among those who say the Great Commission has been misunderstood and misused by Western churches to further their own colonial and commercial agendas. What we today call globalization, she says, is for the indigenous people of Latin America just the latest destructive chapter in a five-hundred-year process that began with the arrival of Christopher Columbus. The church, and by this she means all churches that call themselves Christian, Protestant or otherwise, "has failed the people by becoming part of the institutions of society that oppress. If the church is the presence of God on earth, how can it work with the military and the oligarchs at the expense of the people? The church has become just another transnational country."

For evangelicals, gaining converts is at the heart of the Great Commission. But Benavides aligns herself with those liberal Protestants who say today's pluralistic sensitivities dictate an updated understanding of the Great Commission, one that relies on acts and attitudes that bear witness to the transformative power that flows from living life with an open heart, as they believe Jesus meant for it to be lived. That, says Benavides, is the essence of Jesus' message for the age of "global, predatory capitalism. We must live according to the Christian principles of sharing and co-operation and not look upon people as a commodity."

Benavides became a minister in the 1970s, when she worked with the late Roman Catholic archbishop Oscar

Romero, who was slain by rightists during El Salvador's civil war. Thirty years later she rarely attends church services, preferring to spend quiet time in the countryside. "When I am alone with my spirit, then I am in church," she says. But being alone with nature is becoming ever harder in El Salvador, as elsewhere, as remaining forests are cut for their wood and open fields are given over to housing for her homeland's burgeoning population. "We need to take care of the people, but we also need to take care of the earth. That's what Christians are supposed to do also."

In speaking of her reverence for the natural world, Benavides touches on another biblical principle that informs her attitude toward globalization. It is an injunction many theologically liberal Protestants regard of greater importance today than perhaps ever before. In a word, it is stewardship.

In a Christian context, stewardship refers to the belief that the spirit of God is in all of creation—*His* creation. "Heaven is my throne, and the earth is my footstool.... Has not my hand made all these things?" (Acts 7:49–50).

Stewardship makes it incumbent upon Christians to treat the natural world not as the human environment, but as "God's environment." Immediate attention to wise stewardship, say Benavides and others, is urgently called for because of the worldwide environmental crisis brought on by transnational commercial enterprises that consume huge amounts of natural resources in their insatiable desire for continued material expansion. Stewardship, these Christians say, must take precedent over another, perhaps better known, biblical injunction, "Be fruitful and increase in number; fill the earth and subdue it" (Genesis 1:28).

Judeo-Christian thought is often blamed for the attitude of voraciousness with which market capitalism has sought to fulfill its self-appointed destiny. Jürgen Moltmann, professor emeritus of theology at Germany's University of Tübingen, says that is because ever since the Renaissance the West has identified increasingly with God "the Almighty." Omnipotence became the preferred godly trait. "God is the Lord, the world is God's property, and God can do with it what he likes." From that attitude, it follows that people who consider themselves fashioned in God's image would presume domain over the physical world "in order to prove themselves God's image. Human beings come to resemble their God, not through goodness and truth, not through patience and love, but through power and sovereignty."[14]

Sallie McFague argues that the end result of this thinking is greed, and that Christians—liberal and conservative Protestants, as well as any other kind—are no less prone to greed than anyone else. "To be sure," she says, "Christians do not openly support, 'Blessed are the greedy.' Nonetheless, that is the way most of us live. Why? Quite simply, because we are members of a society, now a worldwide one, that accepts, almost without question, an economic theory that supports insatiable greed on the part of individuals." Rather than continuing in this mode, McFague, a theologian who taught for three decades at Vanderbilt Divinity School, joins Benavides in arguing for an ecologically sustainable theology that rejects consumerism, as well as for a holistic approach recognizing

that "the well-being of the individual is inextricably connected to the well-being of the whole"[15]

McFague's sentiments place her on the Protestant
world's theological left. But as emphasized earlier, such categorizations are inadequate when discussing attitudes
toward globalization. Evangelicals such as Sine and
Goudzwaard speak just as passionately about the need to
defend what's left of the natural environment and its non-
renewable resources from globalization's advance.
Furthermore, they expand the concept of stewardship to
cover the last biblical principle to be considered: justice
and the ethical life.

The biblical God is a just God, and if Christians imagine themselves to be in God's image, then they must strive
to live a just life. "Seek justice, encourage the oppressed,
defend the fatherless, plead the case of the widow," intones
the prophet Isaiah (Isaiah 1:17), while Paul admonishes
Rome's earliest Christians to "share with God's people who
are in need" and "do what is right in the eyes of everybody"
(Romans 12:13, 17).

The concept of biblical justice, "holy justice," is
explained elegantly and most simply by Max L. Stackhouse.
Biblical justice, he says, is a covenantal agreement between
God and God's people, an elevated form of what on the
political level might exist between a feudal overseer and his
peasant population. "X will protect Y, but Y must honor the
edicts of and give tribute to X," in the Stackhouse equation.

It was surely an inspired moment when this basic
"mutual," oath-bound creation of responsible relationships was recognized by some of the ancient

Semitic sages and prophets to be, in revealing ways, a close analogy to the way the one, true righteous and merciful God relates to humanity, and a model of how humans can and should relate to each other under this God. This theological adaptation of the idea shifted it from a matter of the human establishment of peace by domination and subservience, or even a contract of convenience or affection, to an unveiling of the character of a just, merciful God who directly engages in the formation of righteous living in community. A betrayal of that God by human injustice was seen to threaten the well-being of the human partners to the covenant, to the society at large, and even potentially to the creation itself.[16]

Stackhouse goes on to say that despite the covenant, there can be no perfect justice in the world, only an approximation. No person, he says, is fully just, and society is in need of perpetual reform. "Our best justice is the least worst justice," yet Christians remain "called by God to be defenders of the right and active instruments of the good, co-creative covenant partners with God enacting in love, the righteous principles of God, and, in hope, the promises of God as agents of justice."[17]

Ever striving, ever correcting. That, in essence, is the human commitment to the covenantal agreement, a pledge of the soul to remember Jesus' warning that one cannot serve "two masters," that Christians are obligated to choose God over mammon (Matthew 6:24). Moreover, it constitutes recognition that human rights, a notion we moderns like to think is our particular advancement over the ancients, are both transcendent and applicable to all realms—the economic, the political, the interpersonal. Are not human rights explicit in Jesus' words, "in everything, do to others what you would have them do to you, for this sums up the Law and the Prophets" (Matthew 7:12)?

The Protestant churches developed out of what John Witte Jr., director of the law and religion program at Atlanta's Emory University, calls "the second great human rights movement of the West," the Reformation's insistence on freedom of conscience to worship apart from ecclesiastical or state control and by virtue of democratic consensus. At the start of the twenty-first century, Witte argues, the Protestant contribution of human rights tempered by individual responsibility must not be abandoned, and the challenge now for Protestant churches is to translate these theological principles into practical steps that insure just conditions in a globalized world.[18]

The myriad divisions among Protestant churches

coupled with the Protestant inclination toward individual reckoning are likely to prevent any such broad effort, Witte acknowledges. However, it is possible for Protestants professing wildly divergent beliefs to join together on narrower issues. Witness the unprecedented support for the Jubilee 2000 campaign to cancel the international debt of some of the poorest nations. Liberal Protestants aligned with the National Council of Churches of Christ in the U.S.A. made debt relief a priority. Yet high-profile conservatives, including Billy Graham and Pat Robertson, also endorsed the effort (so did the Vatican and a host of non-Christian faith groups, not to mention a Democratic American president and a Republican-controlled Congress). Jubilee 2000 supporters from both ends of the Protestant theological spectrum condemned the crushing Third World debt as a

Protestants professing wildly divergent beliefs can join together on narrower issues. Witness the unprecedented support for the Jubilee 2000 campaign to cancel the international debt of some of the poorest nations. Liberal Protestants aligned with the National Council of Churches of Christ in the USA made debt relief a priority. Yet high-profile conservatives, including Billy Graham and Pat Robertson, also endorsed the effort (so did the Vatican and a host of non-Christian faith groups, not to mention a Democratic American president and a Republican-controlled Congress). Jubilee 2000 supporters from both ends of the Protestant theological spectrum condemned the crushing Third World debt as a manifestation of globalization's downside, while citing the call in Leviticus 25 to forgive debt and return land to its original owners as their biblical motivation.

manifestation of globalization's downside, while citing the call in Leviticus 25 to forgive debt and return land to its original owners as their biblical motivation.

"In its most basic sense," says Witte, globalization is "the process of compressing cultural time and space, of bringing the persons and peoples of the world into increasingly regular interaction."[19] The Protestant world is also being compressed. Still, it's hard to imagine globalization compressing differences to the point where David E. Bay and Marta Benavides will agree on much.

In the end, the question is, how will the Protestant churches handle the accelerating changes and pressures that globalization has heaped, and is still to heap, upon them, amid their differences and in the absence of the final confirmation promised by Scripture? We could see another spurt in middle-ground ecumenism that might attract the likes of Kooperkamp and Sine—social justice liberals and social, if not theological, liberal evangelicals. It would be a bond born of revulsion to injustice and anchored in stewardship. Perhaps the existing group called Evangelicals for Social Action is a harbinger. But don't expect globalization to force union between Protestantism's more strident voices. Until the final confirmation, they will argue their truths, but faith alone remains the only answer. For Protestants, no other justification is needed.

Conclusion:
"Nowherian" Concerns

Pico Iyer—born in England to parents from Bombay, reared in California but sent back to Britain for schooling, and now a Buddhist living in Japan—is a "Global Soul," a member of the international cultural elite about which he writes so eloquently, but with more than a touch of melancholy over what he knows has been lost.

> Growing up, I had no relatives on the same continent as myself, and I never learned a word of my mother's tongue or my father's (because, coming from different parts of India, they had no common language save that of British India). To this day, I can't pronounce what is technically my first name, and the name by which I go is an Italian one.... As a permanent alien, I've never been in a position to vote, and, in fact, I've never held a job in the country where I more or less live.... The son of Hindu-born Theosophists, I was educated entirely in

Christian schools and spend most of my time now in Buddhist lands (the Caribbean islanders would call me a "Nowherian"), and though I spend most of my year in rural Japan or in a Catholic monastery, I've nonetheless accumulated 1.5 million miles on one American airline alone.

Neither exile or expatriate, refugee or nomad, the "state of foreignness" is the closest thing Iyer knows to a real home. His worldliness enables him to live "above parochialisms." But, he notes, that same "displacement can encourage the wrong kinds of distance, and if the nationalism we see sparking up around the globe arises from too narrow and fixed a sense of loyalty, the internationalism that's coming to birth may reflect too roaming and undefined a sense of belonging." Able to see all sides of a question but devoid of fixed convictions, the Global Soul, he says, "may grow so used to giving back a different self according to his environment that he loses sight of who he is when nobody's around."[1]

Iyer may lament his life of flux, but his is still a privileged one with greater than average options when it comes to making decisions about existential issues. The residents of Tambogrande, Peru, on the other hand, have fewer options. They are not Global Souls, but people as rooted in the San Lorenzo Valley's soil as are their fruit trees, which have sustained them for generations.

So when a Canadian mining company came calling and offered new jobs, new homes, and 350 million dollars in project investments, the people of Tambogrande voted nine-to-one against acceptance. They reasoned that the vast majority of the scheme's estimated billion dollars in profits would go to Vancouver-based Manhattan Minerals and to Peru's central government some 540 miles away in Lima, that much of their town would be destroyed by the open-pit mine from which gold would be extracted, and that the project would open the door to further mining operations around their community of twenty thousand people. They chose preserving their homes and way of life over promised, and uncertain, monetary "progress." "In mining zones, poverty is the highest and prostitution the greatest," one resident, Eligio Villegas Salvador, an evangelical Christian, told a visiting journalist.[2]

Home. It's about identity and inner security—that sense of belonging that Iyer craves and Salvador is loath to jeopardize. They may have little else in common, but the two men do share the need for intimacy, community, and commitment that define human existence.

This book quotes at length representatives of the world's faith traditions decrying the lack of economic justice that they see undermining whatever material benefits globalization offers. Meanwhile, the anger among those who perceive themselves to be suffering the injustice builds worldwide. Ironically, it is stoked by the globalization of media, which is largely viewed as a vehicle for Western, primarily American, values. "What America exports to poor countries through the ubiquitous media—pictures of glittering abundance and national self-absorption—enrages those whom it doesn't depress," says the journalist George Packer.[3]

But there is no turning back. Nostalgia for a simpler past (did such a thing ever really exist?) serves no purpose for most other than to ignite the poet's imagination. Romantic images, the poor know best, feed no one. Martin E. Marty, the American scholar of contemporary religious trends (and an ordained Lutheran minister), recounts being reminded of this by a Chilean Jesuit. The priest overheard Marty and others discussing technology's "dehumanizing" effect on traditional cultures. Do you not understand, said the priest, that technology's advances are often welcomed in such cultures because of the "comfort, longer lives, opportunities for leisure activities, [and] convenience" they promise?[4] Case in point: remember the comments of Meitamel Olol-Dapash, the Masai representative? He does not favor walling off his people from globalization. Rather, he seeks ways to preserve what his culture holds most sacred while also participating in the global economy in a way that is advantageous to the Masai. Nor do the people of the San Lorenzo Valley object to selling their fruit on the global market. They want participation, not isolation, while maintaining a way of life that's comfortable in its familiarity. Is Iyer's angst worth the frequent flyer miles?

"Glocalization" is the term many use to explain attempts to blend local values with globalization. Another example of this are the Hindu software technicians in India who offer *puja*, or worship, to their computers draped with garlands, as they would statues of deities.[5] Yet another is the Daudi Bohra Isma'ili Muslim community, a tight-knit, socially conservative group that embraces Western education nonetheless.

As important as economics may be, it is not, as the great religions stress, the full measure of humanity. There is also connection to self, to others, to the ingrained values that have sustained cultures for generations and millennia, and to the belief in transcendence that gives it all meaning. In the end, what unnerves people most about globalization—including many in the West who may fairly be said to be on the winning side (economically, that is) of the process so far—is the threat it poses to that which is most precious to a life of satisfaction: our sense of meaning.

Hinduism offers a paradigm for understanding this. The term *satchidananda* is comprised of three Sanskrit parts. *Sat* may be translated as "being," *chid* as "consciousness," and *ananda* as "bliss." Together, satchidananda sums up what we all want: to continue living, to understand what is happening to us, and to be happy. Everything we do is meant to advance this integrated triad, even if what we do eventually turns out misguided. We act on the assumption that we are not. Globalization's prevailing ethic posits that chit may be

> As important as economics may be, it is not, as the great religions stress, the full measure of humanity. There is also connection to self, to others, to the ingrained values that have sustained cultures for generations and millennia, and to the belief in transcendence that gives it all meaning. In the end, what unnerves people most about globalization—including many in the West who may fairly be said to be on the winning side (economically, that is) of the process so far—is the threat it poses to that which is most precious to a life of satisfaction: our sense of meaning.

reduced to a need for material advancement, from which sat is likely to benefit and ananda, we hope, will follow. Religion's spiritual core holds that chit requires relationship with a higher power, however it is imagined (to borrow from the neutral language of Alcoholics Anonymous), and that without it the body may keep functioning but can never know true bliss. Our worldview determines which of these two perspectives makes greater sense. But in either case, once we reach an understanding of the universe—once we develop a worldview that seems to make sense—the principle of satchidananda says we will cling to it and make it our life. We do so because we are compelled to seek *meaning* or face despair.

But why is it that, as the well-worn cliché informs us, few facing imminent death cry over not having spent more time at the office? Why is it that all the faith traditions examined in this book agree that Michael Douglas's character in the film *Wall Street* got it horribly wrong when he proclaimed, "Greed is good"? Why are mystics worshipped, both figuratively and literally, more than industrialists and entrepreneurs? Consider which of the two human society holds up to represent our noblest aspirations as a species. And why is it that people are willing to put chit before sat, are willing to put principle before life, are willing to die for their beliefs?

Claims about specific truth vary widely. Religions insist that theirs is the clear spiritual vision. It's all further proof of the human need for a sense of transcendent connection, to live in alignment with something that stands in for the larger context. Whether they look toward the stars

Spiritual connection is the core of religious formulation. At the level of daily existence, this connection is expressed through living in community. It is in communion with each other that we come to know who we are, and to gain comfort and support from that knowledge. We all share the need for communal membership, and if the harmful effects of globalization—which is likely to proceed in any event—are to be minimized, the spiritual as well as the material needs of the world's plurality must also be addressed.

or to revealed texts, people seek answers to life's most profound questions, and, once they come up with an answer, cling to it, because understanding imparts purpose beyond that offered by mere existence, which will end in any event, or fleeting happiness, which ebbs and flows with life's daily tides.

The majority of people appear to agree with this assessment,[6] even if their daily activities would seem to indicate they dwell in some post-religious consciousness. Robert N. Bellah, the renowned sociologist of religion, explains this apparent contradiction by noting that "there are *cultural codes* [his emphasis] embedded in national cultures and that these cultural codes, however transformed over time, are ultimately derived from religious beliefs." Moreover, says Bellah, these codes, because they are so deeply engrained in us all and are so taken for granted, "are far less malleable than the fads and fashions that inundate us daily."[7]

Spiritual connection is the core of religious formulation. At the level of daily existence, this connection is expressed through living in community. It is in communion with each other that we come to know who we are, and to gain comfort and support from that knowledge. It is our karma yoga.

Once, in the Ecuadorian jungle, a nomadic Waorani Indian who lived in a hastily constructed thatched-roof hut with his extended family told me that he felt sorry for me when I—rather than try to explain the concepts of divorce and shared child custody—simply said I lived alone. Who would hunt for me if I were hurt? he asked. Who would defend me if I were attacked? A few metal pots and machetes were this man's only material link to the world beyond his forest, but he grasped the importance of connection to others and home at its most vital level. His spirituality was no less profound that than that of a high-church emissary.

This is what the Global Soul loses. This is what those around the world who oppose globalization's Western monoculture fear losing.

We all share the need for communal membership, and if the harmful effects of globalization—which is likely to proceed in any event—are to be minimized, the spiritual as well as the material needs of the world's plurality must also be addressed. The first step is to show respect for these needs. This means respect for the ways that others structure life, for their values and beliefs, and for the land upon which their ways have flourished. It does not mean claiming more territory for Disney and McDonald's[8] in the short run while hoping barbed wire and armaments will keep us safe over the long term—a strategy that too many in the West confuse with genuine globalization.

Robert Wright, the hyper-globalist scholar and author, notes that the writer Dorothy Parker, "when asked if she

enjoyed writing, replied, 'No, I enjoy having written.'"
Globalization, says Wright, may be a similar proposition.
"It could well turn out that having globalized is more fun
than globalizing. Though the ends of globalization are fundamentally good—reducing poverty, nurturing democracy
and freedom—the process of globalizing can be quite costly in human terms, especially when it moves at high veloc-
ity." Globalization could well be a secular approximation of
the messianic vision as Wright and others contend. But as
he admits, the short-term human toll can be quite costly. If
that bothers you, he suggests, contribute to charity.[9]

A religious person would say we can and must do better. Money may buy food, but it does not purchase real
community, and without that sense of connection those
who feel exploited and disrespected get angrier as they
become more alienated from the emerging global culture—
even if they are better off materially than their parents.
Some have found an antidote to this loss of identity in
defensive religion. The evidence of this is all too apparent
in societies where theology has become a weapon against
the loss of control blamed, rightly or wrongly, on globalization's cultural incursion.

Nor does money assuage our responsibility. Various
commentators have said globalization needs a "human
face," "soul," "a level playing field," "more entry points,"
and a "global ethic." Pope John Paul II has urged redefin-
ing the very concept of prosperity to include its social
implications. If we are all accountable to God, says Rabbi
Arthur Waskow, then we are all responsible when transnational corporations cut jobs in Detroit so they may hire

workers in China at a lower wage. As the world continues to compress, as accounting scandals in Texas and Mississippi reverberate in London and Tokyo, globalization's free-market, libertarian values seem to cry out for restraint.

Religion's spiritual and ethical elements can be an answer. "Religion," say Bahá'ís, "provides the bricks and mortar of society—the ethical precepts and vision that unite people into communities and that give tangible direction and meaning to individual and collective existence."[10] For this to happen, though, we need to take seriously what our traditions tell us is of lasting value.

NOTES

Introduction
Why the Passion

1. Serge Schmemann, "Where McDonald's Sits Down with Arab Nationalists," *New York Times*, February 2, 2002, sec. A, p. 10.

2. Benjamin R. Barber, *Jihad vs. McWorld: How Globalism and Tribalism Are Reshaping the World* (New York: Times Books, 1995). Barber is generally credited with coining this phrase now in common use.

3. Edwin A. Locke, "Anti-Globalization: The Left's Violent Assault on Global Prosperity," in CapitalismMagazine.com, http://www.capitalismmagazine.com, May 1, 2002.

4. Joseph E. Stiglitz, *Globalization and Its Discontents* (New York: W.W. Norton & Co., 2002), p. 7.

5. George Soros, *On Globalization* (New York: Public Affairs, 2002), p. 5.

6. Foreign Policy, "Globalization's Last Hurrah? The A.T. Kearney/Foreign Policy Magazine 2000 Globalization Index," no. 128 (January/February 2002), pp. 38–51.

7. Yongzheng Yang and Yiping Huang, "The Impact of Trade Liberalization on Income Distribution in China" (working paper, Research School of Pacific Asian Studies, The Australian National University, Canberra, Australia, 1997).

8. Vatican Information Service, "Globalization Must Not Be a New Form of Colonialism," April 27, 2001.

9. Robert Wright, "Channeling Global Capitalism," in *Slate*, http://slate.msn.com/, June 6, 2002.

10. Huston Smith, *Why Religion Matters: The Fate of the Human Spirit in an Age of Disbelief* (New York: HarperSanFrancisco, 2001), p. 25.

11. David R. Loy, "The West against the Rest? A Response to 'The Clash of Civilizations,'" on the Web site of the Transnational Foundation for Peace and Future Research, http://www.transnational.org/, May 7, 2002.

12. Diana L. Eck, *A New Religious America: How a "Christian Country" Has Now Become the World's Most Religiously Diverse Nation* (New York: HarperSanFrancisco, 2001), p. 24.

Chapter 1
Roman Catholicism: Solidarity in Justice

1. "Roman Catholic" refers to churches and individuals who recognize the pope as head of the universal church and Rome as the center of ecclesiastical authority, including non-Latin-rite churches such as Greek Catholics and Ukrainian Catholics. Not all who call themselves Catholics (i.e., Old Catholics) accept those positions. For simplicity, Catholic when used here refers only to Roman Catholics. Unless otherwise noted, church (or Church if so written by a quoted writer) also refers to the Catholic Church and not the larger Christian church.

2. George Weigel, *Witness to Hope: The Biography of Pope Paul II* (New York: HarperCollins, 1999), p. 846.

3. Hans Küng, *A Global Ethic for Global Politics and Economics* (New York: Oxford University Press, 1998), p. 135.

4. Robert J. Schreiter, *The New Catholicity: Theology between the Global and the Local* (Maryknoll, N.Y.: Orbis Books, 1997), p. 23.

5. Ira Rifkin, "Pope Ends History-Making Pilgrimage to Cuba," Religion News Service, January 25, 1998.

6. Pope John Paul II, "Message of His Holiness Pope John Paul II for the Celebration of the World Day of Peace," January 1, 2000. Available on the Vatican Web site: http://www.vatican.va/.

7. Pope John Paul II, "Encyclical *Laborem Exercens*," September 14, 1981. Available on the Vatican Web site: http://www.vatican.va/.

8. Pope John Paul II, "Encyclical *Sollicitudo Rei Socialis*," December 30, 1987. Available on the Vatican Web site: http://www.vatican.va/.

9. Pope John Paul II, "Encyclical *Centesimus Annus*, May 1, 1991. Available on the Vatican Web site: http://www.vatican.va/.

10. Cardinal Francis George, "How Globalization Challenges the Church's Mission," address at the American Mission Congress, Paraná, Argentina, December 16, 1999. Available at OriginsOnline.com: http://www.originsonline.com/.

11. Anto Akkara, "Globalization Worries Third World Bishops," CatholicWorldNews.com, May 22, 1998; Douglas Todd, "Canadian Bishops Ask Rewrite of NAFTA Environmental Rules," Religion News Service, February 20, 2002.

12. George Weigel, "Papacy and Power," *First Things*, no. 110 (February 2001), p. 18.

13. Rich Heffern, "Thomas Berry: Earth's Crisis is Fundamentally Spiritual," in *National Catholic Reporter* 37, no. 36 (August 10, 2001), p. 3.

14. Küng, p. 135.

15. Kenneth Himes, "Globalization's Next Phase" (address given at Boston College, April 18, 2002). Available at OriginsOnline.com: http://www.originsonline.com/.

16. "Global Issues," Caritas Internationalis Web site: http://www.caritas.org/.

17. Ian Gary, "Africa's Churches Wake to Oil's Problems and Possibilities," *Association of Concerned African Scholars Bulletin*, no. 60/61 (Fall 2001).

18. Martin Wroe, "An Irresistible Force," *Sojourners*

Magazine 29, no. 3 (May-June 2000), p. 18.

19. Pope John Paul II, "Message of the Holy Father to the Group 'Jubilee 2000 Debt Campaign,'" September 23, 1999. Available on the Vatican Web site: http://www.vatican.va/.

20. Philip Jenkins, *The Next Christendom: The Coming of Global Christianity* (New York: Oxford University Press, 2002), pp. 213–14.

21. Tissa Balasuriya, *Globalization and Human Solidarity* (Thiruvalla, Kerala, India: Christava Sahitya Samithy, 2000), p. 72.

22. "Catholic Intellectuals War of Alignment with Anti-Globalization," Zenit.org, July 5, 2001.

23. Richard John Neuhaus, "The Public Square," *First Things*, no. 116 (October 2001), p. 71, and no. 100 (February 2000), p. 77.

Chapter 2
Islam: God as History

1. President Guy Verhofstadt of Belgium used this term during the World Economic Forum's 2002 meeting in New York.

2. Ameer Ali, "Globalization and Greed: A Muslim Perspective," in *Subverting Greed: Religious Perspectives on the Global Economy,* edited by Paul F. Knitter and Chandra Muzaffar (Boston: Boston Research Center for the 21st Century, 2002), p. 140.

3. Ali, p. 146.

4. Huston Smith, *The Illustrated World's Religions: A Guide to Our Wisdom Traditions,* 2d ed. (New York: HarperSan-Franciso, 1995), p. 177.

5. Karen Armstrong, *Islam: A Short History* (New York: Modern Library, 2000), p. xi.

6. Armstrong, p. 6.

7. Fathi Osman, *Concepts of the Quran: A Topical Reading* (Los Angeles: MVI Publications, 1997), p. 787.

8. Ibrahim M. Abu-Rabi', "Globalization: A Contemporary Islamic Response," *American Journal of Islamic Social Sciences* 15, no. 3 (Fall 1998), p. 30.

9. M. A. Muqtedar Khan, "Constructing Identity in 'Glocal' Politics," *American Journal of Islamic Social Sciences* 15, no. 3 (Fall 1998), p. 100.

10. M. A. Muqtedar Khan, "Muslim to Muslim," *Christian Century*, November 7, 2001, p. 5.

11. Ali A. Mazrui, "Globalization, Islam and the West," *American Journal of Islamic Social Sciences* 15, no. 3 (Fall 1998), pp. 9–12.

12. Thomas L. Friedman, "Iran's Third Wave," *New York Times*, June 16, 2002, sec. 4, p. 13.

13. Aga Khan, from a speech given at the Conference on Indigenous Philanthropy, Islamabad, Pakistan, October 16–17, 2000, available at: http://www.akdn.org/agency/philanthropy/ingphilHHADD.html.

14. Syedna Muhammad Burhanuddin, quoted by Jonah Blank, *Mullahs on the Mainframe: Islam and Modernity among the Daudi Bohras* (Chicago: University of Chicago Press, 2001), p. 3.

15. Jonah Blank, *Mullahs on the Mainframe: Islam and Modernity among the Daudi Bohras* (Chicago: University of Chicago Press, 2001), pp. 1–2.

Chapter 3
Hinduism: Creating Global Karma

1. Adherents.com: http://www.adherents.com/adh_branches.html#Hinduism.

2. Tulasi Srinivas, "A Tryst with Destiny: The Indian Case of Cultural Globalization," in *Many Globalizations: Cultural Diversity in the Contemporary World*, edited by Peter L. Berger and Samuel P. Huntington (New York: Oxford University Press, 2002), p. 110.

3. Daniel Yergin, "Giving Aid to World Trade," *New York Times*, June 27, 2002, sec. A, p. 29.

4. Huston Smith, *The Illustrated World's Religions: A Guide to Our Wisdom Traditions*, 2d ed. (New York: HarperSanFrancisco, 1995), p. 18.

5. Smith, p. 22.

6. Keith Crim, ed., *Abingdon Dictionary of Living Religions* (Nashville: Abingdon, 1981), p. 460.

7. Swami Agnivesh, "Religious Conscience and the Global Economy: An Eastern Perspective on Socio-Spiritual Activism," in *Subverting Greed: Religious Perspectives on the Global Economy*, edited by Paul F. Knitter and Chandra Muzaffar (Boston: Boston Research Center for the 21st Century, 2002), pp. 44, 46, and 47.

8. Agnivesh, p. 53.

9. Agnivesh, p. 48.

10. Vasudha Narayanan, quoted by M. P. Mohanty in "India's Ecological Mess," *Hinduism Today* 21, no. 5 (May 1999), p. 16.

11. Mahatma Gandhi, July 6, 1919. Available on the Web site of India's Ministry of External Affairs: http://meadev.nic.in/Gandhi/swadeshi.htm.

12. Vasuki (C. Abraham Varghese), *Cultural Nationalism vis-à-vis Multinationals* (Mumbai: Hindu Vivek Kendra, 1996).

13. Smith, p. 52.

14. Vinay Lal, "Reflections on the Indian Diaspora, in the Caribbean and Elsewhere," Manas Web site: http://www.sscnet.ucla.edu/southasia/index.html.

15. Lal. "Reflections on the Indian Diaspora, in the Caribbean and Elsewhere."

Chapter 4
Judaism: Speaking Truth to Power

1. YHWH, a contraction consisting of the four consonants of the English name of the Biblical deity, is a common Jewish way of writing the sacred name of God, which Jewish law prohibits writing or pronouncing in its entirety.

2. Avi Beker, *Dispersion and Globalization: The Jews and the International Economy* (Jerusalem: Institute of the World Jewish Congress, 2001), p. 19.

3. Geoffrey Wigoder, ed., *The Encyclopedia of Judaism* (New York: Macmillan Publishing Company, 1989), p. 247.

4. Beker, p. 13.

5. Beker, p. 17.

6. Beker, p. 4.

7. Union of Councils for Jews in the Former Soviet Union, *Holocaust Deniers Hold Conference in Moscow,* media statement, Washington, D.C., January 30, 2002. The statement notes that "cosmopolitan" is a Stalin-era code word for Jews. "Talmudists" refers to the Talmud, Judaism's authoritative body of law and lore.

8. Manny Fernandez, "Demonstrators Rally to Palestinian Cause: Arab Americans, Supporters Drown Out Other Issues," *Washington Post,* April 21, 2002, p. 1.

9. Commission on Social Action of Reform Judaism, "Proposed Resolution on International Trade," (presented at the Union of American Hebrew Congregations' 66th Biennial Convention, Boston, Dececember 5–9, 2001).

10. Rabbi David Seidenberg, *In Every Generation—The Pesach Seder of Globalization, the Rich & the Poor,* available at the Web site of the Shalom Center: http://www.shalomctr.org/, Philadelphia, 2002.

11. Michael Lerner, *Spirit Matters* (Charlottesville, Va.: Hampton Roads Publishing, 2000), p. 5.

12. Wigoder, *The Encyclopedia of Judaism,* p. 392.

Chapter 5
Buddhism: Bodhisattvas in Boardrooms

1. David R. Loy, "Pave the Planet or Wear Shoes? A Buddhist Perspective on Greed and Globalization," in *Subverting Greed: Religious Perspectives on the Global Economy*, edited by Paul F. Knitter and Chandra Muzaffar (Boston: Boston Research Center for the 21st Century, 2002), p. 65.

2. Charles Prebish, "The Buddhist Landscape," *Shambhala Sun* 10, no. 4 (March 2002), p. 46.

3. Thich Nhat Hanh, "The Sun My Heart," in *Dharma Rain: Sources of Buddhist Environmentalism*, edited by Stephanie Kaza and Kenneth Kraft (Boston: Shambhala Publications, 2000), p. 84.

4. Dalai Lama, *Ethics for the New Millennium* (New York: Riverhead Books, 1999), pp. 161–62.

5. See Nancy Jack Todd, "E. F. Schumacher: An Appreciation," in *People, Land, and Community: Collected E. F. Schumacher Society Lectures*, edited by Hildegarde Hannum, with annotations by Nancy Jack Todd (New Haven: Yale University Press, 1997).

6. Loy, p. 71.

7. I am indebted to David R. Loy for my understanding of this distinction. Any misunderstanding is my responsibility.

8. Robert Aitken, "Envisioning the Future," in *Dharma Rain*, p. 424.

9. Sulak Sivaraksa, "Development As if People Mattered," in *Dharma Rain*, p. 189.

10. Jane Hurst, "Nichiren Shoshu and Soka Gakkai in America: The Pioneer Spirit," in *The Faces of Buddhism in America*, edited by Charles S. Prebish and Kenneth K. Tanaka (Berkeley and Los Angeles: University of California Press, 1998), p. 89.

11. Bryan Wilson, "The British Movement and Its Members," in *Global Citizens: The Soka Gakkai Buddhist Movement in*

the World, edited by David Machacek and Bryan Wilson (Oxford: Oxford University Press, 2000), p. 357.

12. Daisaku Ikeda, "The SGI Peace Movement," in *Buddhist Peacework: Creating Cultures of Peace,* edited by David W. Chappell (Somerville, Mass.: Wisdom Publications, 1999), p. 136.

13. Dalai Lama, p. 131.

Chapter 6
Bahá'í Faith: One for All

1. Shoghi Effendi, *The World Order of Bahá'u'llá* (Wilmette, Ill.: Bahá'í Publishing Trust, 1938), p. 202.

2. City Montessori School Web site: http://www.cmseducation. org/wrlcitizen.htm.

3. Effendi, p. 202.

4. Bahá'u'lláh, *Gleanings from the Writings of the Bahá'u'lláh,* 2d rev. ed. (Wilmette, Ill.: Bahá'í Publishing Trust, 1976), p. 215.

5. Bahá'í International Community, Office of Public Information, *Turning Point for All Nations* (Haifa: Bahá'í World Centre, 1995), p. 20.

6. Bahá'í International Community, Office of Public Information, *Who Is Writing the Future? Reflections on the Twentieth Century,* February 1999. Available at: http://www.bahai.org/article-1-7-3-1.html.

7. U.S. Department of State, Bureau of Democracy, Human Rights, and Labor, *2000 Annual Report on International Religious Freedom: Iran (*September 5, 2000).

8. Bahá'í International Community, *Who Is Writing the Future?*

9. Bahá'u'lláh, quoted in *One Country: Newsletter of the Bahá'í International Community* 9, no. 2 (July-September 1997), p. 3.

10. Bahá'í International Community, Office of Public Information, *The Prosperity of Humankind* (January 1995), pp. 6–7.

11. Bahá'í International Community, *The Prosperity of Humankind*, p. 7.

12. Bahá'í International Community, *The Prosperity of Humankind*, p. 8.

13. Bahá'í International Community, *The Prosperity of Humankind*, p. 11.

Chapter 7
Tribal and Earth-Based Religions:
In Defense of the Mother

1. Huston Smith, *The Illustrated World's Religions: A Guide to Our Wisdom Traditions*, 2d ed. (New York: HarperSanFrancisco, 1995), p. 232.

2. John A. Grim, "Indigenous Traditions and Ecology," *Earth Ethics* 10, no. 1 (Fall/Winter 1998). Available on the Web site of the Forum on Religion and Ecology: http://environment.harvard.edu/religion/research/indhome.html.

3. Steve Twomey, "An Unnatural Journey for Nature's Cause: Leaders of U'wa Tribe See Protests as a Fight for the Simple Life," *Washington Post*, April 20, 2001, p. B3.

4. Erin Fitzhenry, "The Embodiment of Enkai: The Mau Forest and Maasai Spirituality," *Cultural Survival Voices* 1, no. 3 (summer 2002), p. 8.

5. Ifi Amadiume, "Igbo and African Religious Perspectives on Religious Conscience and the Global Economy," in *Subverting Greed: Religious Perspectives on the Global Economy*, edited by Paul F. Knitter and Chandra Muzaffar (Boston: Boston Research Center for the 21st Century, 2002), pp. 20, 23.

6. Amadiume, p. 32.

7. Starhawk, *The Spiral Dance: A Rebirth of the Ancient Religion of the Great Goddess*, 3d ed. (New York: HarperSanFrancisco, 1999), p. 16.

8. Margot Adler, "A Time for Truth: Wiccans Struggle with Information That Revisions Their History," Beliefnet.com, http://beliefnet.com/, 2000.

9. Starhawk, p. 29.

10. Starhawk, p. 7.

11. Starhawk, p. 36.

12. Joseph Campbell, *The Way of the Animal Powers, Vol. 1, Historical Atlas of World Mythology* (London: Summerfield Press, 1983), p. 73.

Chapter 8
Protestantism: Going by the Book

1. David Chidester, *Christianity: A Global History* (New York: HarperSanFrancisco, 2000), p. 27.

2. Tom Sine, *Mustard Seed versus McWorld: Reinventing Life and Faith for the Future* (Grand Rapids, Mich.: Baker Books, 1999), p. 19.

3. James W. Skillen, in the introduction to *Globalization and the Kingdom of God (The Kuyper Lecture Series)*, by Bob Goudzwaard, edited by Skillen, with responses by Brian Fikkert, Larry Reed, and Adolfo García de la Sienra, The Center for Public Justice (Grand Rapids, Mich.: Baker Books, 2001), p. 19.

4. Goudzwaard, p. 20.

5. Tom Sine, "Who is Tim LaHaye?," *Sojourners Magazine* (September-October 2001).

6. David Barrett, quoted by Mark Hutchinson in "Globalization Is Changing How Christians Do Ministry," *Christianity Today* 42, no. 13 (November 16, 1998), p. 46.

7. Sine, p. 76.

8. Goudzwaard, *Globalization and the Kingdom of God*, p. 19.

9. Max L. Stackhouse, in the introduction to *God and Globalization: Religion and the Powers of the Common Life*, vol. 1, edited by Max L. Stackhouse and Peter J. Paris (Harrisburg, Penn.: Trinity Press International, 2000), p. 20.

10. James Kurth, "Religion and Globalization" (lecture given at the Foreign Policy Research Institute, Philadelphia, April 7, 1998). Edited version available at: http://www.fpri.org.

11. Philip Jenkins, *The Next Christendom: The Coming of Global Christianity* (New York: Oxford University Press, 2002), p. 6.

12. Jenkins, p. 8.

13. Quoted by Alex Duval Smith in "The South Set to Export Gospel to Northern Hemisphere," *Ecumenical News International* (July 12, 2001).

14. Jürgen Moltmann, "The Destruction and Healing of the Earth," in *God and Globalization: The Spirit and the Modern Authorities*, vol. 2 edited by Max L. Stackhouse and Don S. Browning, (Harrisburg, Penn.: Trinity Press International, 2001), p. 173.

15. Sallie McFague, "God's Household: Christianity, Economics, and Planetary Living," in *Subverting Greed: Religious Perspectives on the Global Economy*, edited by Paul F. Knitter and Chandra Muzaffar (Boston: Boston Research Center for the 21st Century, 2002), pp. 120, 126.

16. Max L. Stackhouse, "Covenantal Justice in a Global Era" (lecture given at the Institute for Reformed Theology, Richmond, Virginia, September 22, 2000). Available at: http://www.reformedtheology.org.

17. Stackhouse, "Covenantal Justice in a Global Era."

18. John Witte Jr., "The Spirit of the Law, the Laws of the Spirit," in Stackhouse and Browning, *God and Globalization*, p. 98.

19. Witte, p. 76.

Conclusion
"Nowherian" Concerns

1. Pico Iyer, *The Global Soul: Jet Lag, Shopping Malls and the Search for Home* (New York: Alfred A. Knopf, 2000), pp. 23–25.

2. Scott Wilson, "A Life Worth More than Gold: A Peruvian Town Tries to Turn Away Mining Company," *Washington Post*, June 9, 2002, sec. A, p. 1.

3. George Packer, "When Here Sees There," *New York Times Magazine*, April 21, 2002, sec. 6, p. 13.

4. Martin E. Marty, "Quotidian Acts," *Christian Century* 119, no. 14 (July 3–10, 2002), p. 47.

5. Peter L. Berger and Samuel P. Huntington, eds., *Many Globalizations: Cultural Diversity in the Contemporary World* (New York: Oxford University Press, 2002), p. 110.

6. Adherents.com estimates that 86 percent of the world population self-identifies as being connected to some religious tradition, while 14 percent self-identifies as "nonreligious," a category including atheists, agnostics, secular humanists, and individuals who respond "none" when asked their religious affiliation. See http://www.adherents.com.

7. Robert N. Bellah, "The Protestant Structure of American Culture: Multiculture or Monoculture?" *Hedgehog Review* 4, no. 1 (Spring 2002).

8. I owe this phrase to William Bole.

9. Robert Wright, "Will Globalization Make You Happy?" *Foreign Policy*, no. 120 (September-October 2000), p. 54.

10. "Corruption and Moral Renovation," *One Country: Newsletter of the Bahá'í International Community* 13, no. 4 (January-March 2002), p. 3.

LIST OF INTERVIEWS

The following individuals were interviewed in person, by telephone, or via e-mail by the author.

Introduction: Why the Passion

Janet Dorman, Bonnie Phelps.

Chapter 1
Roman Catholicism: Solidarity in Justice

William Bole, Therese J. Borchard, Sister Judy Cannon, Marie Dennis, Ian Gary, Francis X. Maier, Robert Waldrop.

Chapter 2
Islam: God as History

Hatem Bazian, Bilal El-Amine, Sayyid M. Syeed.

Chapter 3
Hinduism: Creating Global Karma

Anuttama Dasa, B. T. Swami Krishnapada, Yash Malhotra, Sandeep Mody, Sudeep Roy, Vamadeva Shastri.

Chapter 4
Judaism: Speaking Truth to Power

Rabbi Michael Feinberg, Rabbi Barry Freundel, Rabbi Michael Lerner, Mark Pelavin, Rabbi David Seidenberg, Dara Silverman, Rabbi Arthur Waskow.

Chapter 5
Buddhism: Bodhisattvas in Boardrooms

Les Kaye, Kenneth Kraft, David R. Loy, Sybille Scholz, Virginia Straus.

Chapter 6
Bahá'í Faith: One for All

Peter Adriance, Kit Cosby, Bani Dugal, Jagdish Gandhi, W. Andy Knight, Rebequa Getahoun Murphy.

Chapter 7
Tribal and Earth-Based Religions: In Defense of the Mother

Ifi Amadiume, Fritz Jung, John M. Morris, Meitamel Olol-Dapash, Seydina Senghor, Starhawk.

Chapter 8
Protestantism: Going by the Book

David E. Bay, Rev. Marta Benavides, Philip Jenkins, Rev. Earl Kooperkamp, Tom Sine.

FOR FURTHER READING

American Journal of Islamic Social Scientists. *Globalization* 15, no. 3. Herndon, Va.: Association of Muslim Social Scientists, 1998.

Anderson, Walter Truett. *All Connected Now: Life in the First Global Civilization*. Boulder, Co.: Westview Press, 2001.

Appadurai, Arjun. *Modernity at Large: Cultural Dimensions of Globalization*. Minneapolis: University of Minnesota Press, 1996.

———, ed. *Globalization: Millennial Quartet*. Durham, N.C.: Duke University Press, 2000.

Balasuriya, Father Tissa. *Globalization and Human Solidarity*. Thiruvalla, Kerala, India: Christiava Sahitya Samithy, 2000.

Barber, Benjamin R. *Jihad vs. McWorld: How Globalism and Tribalism Are Reshaping the World*. New York: Ballantine Books, 1996.

Beker, Avi. *Dispersion and Globalization: The Jews and the International Economy*. Jerusalem: Institute of the World Jewish Congress, 2001.

Berger, Peter L., and Samuel P. Huntington, eds. *Many Globalizations: Cultural Diversity in the Contemporary World*. New York: Oxford University Press, 2002.

Bhagwati, Jagdish. *The Wind of the Hundred Days: How Washington Mismanaged Globalization*. Cambridge, Mass.: MIT Press, 2000.

Blank, Jonah. *Mullah on the Mainframe: Islam and Modernity among the Daudi Bohras*. Chicago: University of Chicago Press, 2001.

Castles, Stephen, and Mark J. Miller *The Age of Migration: International Population Movements in the Modern World*. New York: Guilford Press, 1993.

Chidester, David. *Christianity: A Global History*. New York: HarperSanFrancisco, 2000.

Chomsky, Noam. *Profit over People: Neoliberalism and Global Order*. New York: Seven Stories Press, 1999.

Diamond, Jared. *Guns, Germs, and Steel: The Fates of Human Societies*. New York: W. W. Norton & Co., 1997.

Dalai Lama [Tenzin Gyatso]. *Ethics for the New Millennium*. New York: Riverhead Books, 1999.

De Vries, Barend. *Champions of the Poor: The Economic Consequences of Judeo-Christian Values*. Washington, D.C.: Georgetown University Press, 1998.

Eck, Diana L. *A New Religious America: How a "Christian Nation" Has Now Become the World's Most Religiously Diverse Nation*. New York: HarperSanFrancisco, 2001.

Friedman, Thomas L. *The Lexus and the Olive Tree: Understanding Globalization* Rev. ed. New York: Anchor Books, 2000.

Goudzwaard, Bob. *Globalization and the Kingdom of God.* Grand Rapids, Mich.: Baker Books, 2001.

Gray, John. *False Dawn: The Delusions of Global Capitalism.* New York: The New Press, 2000.

Greider, William. *One World, Ready or Not: The Manic Logic of Global Capitalism.* New York: Simon & Schuster, 1998.

Hardt, Michael, and Antonio Negri. *Empire.* Cambridge: Harvard University Press, 2000.

Hertz, Noreena. *The Silent Takeover: Global Capitalism and the Death of Democracy.* New York: Free Press, 2001.

Huntington, Samuel P. *The Clash of Civilizations and the Remaking of World Order.* New York: Simon & Schuster, 1996.

International Monetary Fund Staff. *Globalization: Threat or Opportunity?* Issues Briefs no. 00/01. Washington, D.C.: International Monetary Fund. Originally published April 12, 2000; corrected January 2002. Available at: http://www.imf.org/external/np/exr/ib/2000/041200.htm.

Iyer, Pico. *The Global Soul: Jet Lag, Shopping Malls, and the Search for Home.* New York: Alfred A. Knopf, 2000.

Jameson, Fredric, and Masao Miyoshi, eds. *The Cultures of Globalization.* Durham, N.C.: Duke University Press, 1998.

Jenkins, Jerry B., and Tim LaHaye. *Are We Living in the End Times? Current Events Foretold in Scripture...and What They Mean.* Wheaton, Ill.: Tyndale House Publishers, 1999.

Jenkins, Philip. *The Next Christendom: The Coming Global Christianity.* New York: Oxford University Press, 2002.

Kaza, Stephanie, and Kenneth Kraft, eds. *Dharma Rain: Sources of Buddhist Environmentalism.* Boston: Shambhala, 2000.

King, Anthony D., ed. *Culture, Globalization and the World-System: Contemporary Conditions for the Representation of Identity.* Minneapolis: University of Minnesota Press, 1997.

King, Robert Harlen. *Thomas Merton and Thich Nhat Hanh: Engaged Spirituality in an Age of Globalization.* New York: Continuum Publication Group, 2001.

Knitter, Paul F., and Chandra Muzaffar, eds. *Subverting Greed: Religious Perspectives on the Global Economy.* Maryknoll, N.Y.: Orbis Books, 2002.

Korten, David. *When Corporations Rule the World.* 2d ed. Bloomfield, Conn.: Kumarian Press, 2001.

Küng, Hans, *A Global Ethic for Global Politics and Economics.* New York: Oxford University Press, 1998.

———, ed. *Yes to a Global Ethic.* New York: Continuum Publication Group, 1996.

Larsson, Tomas. *The Race to the Top: The Real Story of Globalization.* Washington, D.C.: Cato Institute, 2001.

Lerner, Michael. *The Politics of Meaning: Restoring Hope and Possibility in an Age of Cynicism.* Reading, Mass.: Addison Wesley, 1996.

———. *Spirit Matters: Global Healing and the Wisdom of the Soul.* Charlottesville, Va.: Hampton Roads, 2000.

Lindsey, Brink. *Against the Dead Hand: The Uncertain Struggle for Global Capitalism.* Hoboken, N.J.: John Wiley & Sons, 2001.

Machacek, David, and Bryan Wilson, eds. *Global Citizens: The Soka Gakkai Buddhist Movement in the World.* New York: Oxford University Press, 2000.

Mandelbaum, Michael. *The Ideas that Conquered the World: Peace, Democracy, and Free Markets in the Twenty-First Century.* New York: Public Affairs, 2002.

Mander, Jerry, and Edward Goldsmith. *The Case against the Global Economy—And a Turn toward the Local.* San Francisco: Sierra Club Books, 1996.

Nader, Ralph, ed. *The Case against "Free Trade": GATT, NAFTA, and the Globalization of Corporate Power.* Berkeley, Calif.: North Atlantic Books, 1993.

Palast, Greg. *The Best Democracy Money Can Buy: An Investigative Reporter Exposes the Truth about Globalization, Corporate Cons, and High Finance Fraudsters.* London: Pluto Press, 2002.

Poloma, Margaret M. "The Spirit Bade Me Go: Pentecostalism and Global Religion." Paper presented at the annual meeting of the Association for the

Sociology of Religion, Washington, D.C., August 11–13, 2000. Available at: http://www.hirr.hartsem.edu/research/research_pentecostalism_palomaart1.html.

Postrel, Virginia I. *The Future and Its Enemies: The Growing Conflict over Creativity, Enterprise and Progress.* New York: Simon & Schuster, 1999.

Robertson, Pat. *The New World Order.* Dallas: Word, 1991.

Rodrik, Dani. *Has Globalization Gone Too Far?* Washington: Institute for International Economics, 1997.

Schreiter, Robert J. *The New Catholicity: Theology Between the Global and the Local.* Maryknoll, N.Y.: Orbis Books, 1997.

Sides, Patti M. "Recasting Globalization." Interview with Vittorio Falsina. *Newsletter of the Boston Research Center for the 21st Century,* no. 17 (spring-summer 2001) 6–7, 14–15.

Sine, Tom. *Mustard Seed versus McWorld: Reinventing Life and Faith for the Future.* Grand Rapids, Mich.: Baker Books, 1999.

Soros, George. *On Globalization.* New York: Public Affairs, 2002.

Srinivas, Smriti. *Landscapes of Urban Memory: The Sacred and the Civic in India's High-Tech City.* Minneapolis: University of Minnesota Press, 2001.

Stackhouse, Max L., with Peter J. Paris, eds. *God and Globalization, Vol. 1: Religion and the Powers of the Common Life.* Harrisburg, Penn.: Trinity Press International, 2000.

Stackhouse, Max L., with Don J. Browning, eds. *God and Globalization, Vol. 2: The Spirit and the Modern Authorities.* Harrisburg, Penn.: Trinity Press International, 2001.

Stackhouse, Max L., with Diane B. Obenchain, eds. *God and Globalization, Vol. 3: Christ and the Dominions of Civilization.* Harrisburg, Penn.: Trinity Press International, 2002.

Starhawk. *The Spiral Dance: A Rebirth of the Ancient Religion of the Great Goddess.* 3d ed. New York: HarperSanFrancisco, 1999.

———. *Webs of Power: Notes from the Global Uprising.* Gabriola Island, B.C.: New Society Publishers, 2002.

Stiglitz, Joseph E. *Globalization and Its Discontents* New York: W. W. Norton, 2002.

Taub, William K. *The Amoral Elephant: Globalization and the Struggle for Social Justice in the Twenty-First Century.* New York: Monthly Review Press, 2001.

Wright, Robert. *Nonzero: The Logic of Human Destiny.* New York: Pantheon Books, 2000.

Yergin, Daniel, and Joseph Stanislaw. *The Commanding Heights: The Battle between Government and the Marketplace That Is Remaking the Modern World.* New York: Simon & Schuster, 1998.

Zweig, Michael, ed. *Religion and Economic Justice.* Philadelphia: Temple University Press, 1991.

ACKNOWLEDGMENTS

This book came about as a result of a suggestion by my publisher and editors, and to them I owe a debt of gratitude. Thank you Stuart M. Matlins and Jon M. Sweeney—and thank you Maura D. Shaw, whose calm professionalism provided great support when the task seemed most unmanageable.

Many others helped along the way by providing advice, sources, ideas, books, articles, shelter, encouragement, and friendship. They include Peter Adriance, Bill Aiken, William Bole, Therese J. Borchard, Henry Carrigan, Jr., Kit Cosby, Anuttama Dasa, Fritz Jung, Robert Heller, the Reverend Earl Kooperkamp, Kenneth Kraft, Jon Lowet, David R. Loy, Arthur J. Magida, Patti M. Marxsen, Francis X. Meir, Abby Rosen, Leila Sein, Seydina Senghor, Sybille Scholtz, and Rabbi Arthur Waskow. Thank you as well to all those who consented to interviews; some are included here but far more are listed elsewhere in this book. Additionally, I owe much to the many writers who tackled the subject of globalization before me. I relied heavily on their work, for which I am grateful. Their names may be found in the endnotes or in the list for further reading. The help I received from all was invaluable, but any errors of omission or commission are of course mine alone, and for them I apologize.

I also need to acknowledge the support of my parents, Sylvia and Jack Rifkin, who gave me a start and then let me find my own way. I miss you, Dad, and appreciate what you did for us more each day. To my sister, Trudi Lebowitz, a big fat thank you for all your love. Also, Arno and Rose Boritzer, who have given me so much for so long.

And to all the writers and editors with whom I have had the honor of crossing paths over a long and meandering career, you are far too numerous to list but I am thankful that you shared your skills and made me feel a colleague. I am proud to have worked with some of the best. Lastly, to Baba for setting me on the path, and to Schwartzie for helping me see that the path can be circular.

INDEX

politics and, 139–140, 139–140
Starhawk and, 131, 132, 139,
140–141, 142, 143
Witches and, 131, 141
Wilson, Bryan, 109
Witte, John, Jr., 167–168, 169
World Bank, 4
Catholic influence on, 34
origin of, 5
Protestant view of, 152

World Economic Forum (WEF),
2–3, 146
World Jewish Congress (WJC), 82
World Trade Center, 2, 12, 52, 96
World Trade Organization
(WTO), 4, 86
Wright, Robert, 12, 177–178

Y

Yergin, Daniel, 3, 63

About SKYLIGHT PATHS Publishing

SkyLight Paths Publishing is creating a place where people of different spiritual traditions come together for challenge and inspiration, a place where we can help each other understand the mystery that lies at the heart of our existence.

Through spirituality, our religious beliefs are increasingly becoming a part of our lives—rather than *apart* from our lives. While many of us may be more interested than ever in spiritual growth, we may be less firmly planted in traditional religion. Yet, we do want to deepen our relationship to the sacred, to learn from our own as well as from other faith traditions, and to practice in new ways.

SkyLight Paths sees both believers and seekers as a community that increasingly transcends traditional boundaries of religion and denomination—people wanting to learn from each other, *walking together, finding the way.*

We at SkyLight Paths take great care to produce beautiful books that present meaningful spiritual content in a form that reflects the art of making high quality books. Therefore, we want to acknowledge those who contributed to the production of this book.

PRODUCTION
Sara Dismukes, Tim Holtz,
Martha McKinney & Bridgett Taylor

EDITORIAL
Rebecca Castellano, Amanda Dupuis, Polly Short Mahoney,
Lauren Seidman, Maura D. Shaw & Emily Wichland

COVER DESIGN
Tim Holtz

TEXT DESIGN
Bridgett Taylor
Kristin Goble, PerfecType, Nashville, Tennessee

PRINTING & BINDING
Versa Press, East Peoria, Illinois

Other Interesting Books—Spirituality

Lighting the Lamp of Wisdom: *A Week Inside a Yoga Ashram*
by *John Ittner;* Foreword by *Dr. David Frawley*

This insider's guide to Hindu spiritual life takes you into a typical week of retreat inside a yoga ashram to demystify the experience and show you what to expect from your own visit. Includes a discussion of worship services, meditation and yoga classes, chanting and music, work practice, and more.

6 x 9, 192 pp, b/w photographs, Quality PB, ISBN 1-893361-52-7 **$15.95**; HC, ISBN 1-893361-37-3 **$24.95**

Waking Up: *A Week Inside a Zen Monastery*
by *Jack Maguire;* Foreword by *John Daido Loori, Roshi*

An essential guide to what it's like to spend a week inside a Zen Buddhist monastery.

6 x 9, 224 pp, b/w photographs, HC, ISBN 1-893361-13-6 **$21.95**

Making a Heart for God: *A Week Inside a Catholic Monastery*
by *Dianne Aprile;* Foreword by *Brother Patrick Hart, OCSO*

This essential guide to experiencing life in a Catholic monastery takes you to the Abbey of Gethsemani—the Trappist monastery in Kentucky that was home to author Thomas Merton—to explore the details. "More balanced and informative than the popular *The Cloister Walk* by Kathleen Norris." —*Choice: Current Reviews for Academic Libraries*

6 x 9, 224 pp, b/w photographs, Quality PB, ISBN 1-893361-49-7 **$16.95**; HC, ISBN 1-893361-14-4 **$21.95**

Come and Sit: *A Week Inside Meditation Centers*
by *Marcia Z. Nelson;* Foreword by *Wayne Teasdale*

The insider's guide to meditation in a variety of different spiritual traditions. Traveling through Buddhist, Hindu, Christian, Jewish, and Sufi traditions, this essential guide takes you to different meditation centers to meet the teachers and students and learn about the practices, demystifying the meditation experience.

6 x 9, 224 pp, b/w photographs, Quality PB, ISBN 1-893361-35-7 **$16.95**

Or phone, fax, mail or e-mail to: SKYLIGHT PATHS Publishing
Sunset Farm Offices, Route 4 • P.O. Box 237 • Woodstock, Vermont 05091
Tel: (802) 457-4000   Fax: (802) 457-4004   www.skylightpaths.com
Credit card orders: (800) 962-4544 (8:30AM–5:30PM ET Monday–Friday)
Generous discounts on quantity orders. SATISFACTION GUARANTEED. Prices subject to change.

Spirituality

Who Is My God?
An Innovative Guide to Finding Your Spiritual Identity
Created by *the Editors at SkyLight Paths*

Spiritual Type™ + Tradition Indicator = Spiritual Identity

Your Spiritual Identity is an undeniable part of who you are—whether you've thought much about it or not. This dynamic resource provides a helpful framework to begin or deepen your spiritual growth. Start by taking the unique Spiritual Identity Self-Test™; tabulate your results; then explore one, two, or more of twenty-eight faiths/spiritual paths followed in America today. "An innovative and entertaining way to think—and rethink—about your own spiritual path, or perhaps even to find one." —Dan Wakefield, author of *How Do We Know When It's God?*
6 x 9, 160 pp, Quality PB, ISBN 1-893361-08-X **$15.95**

Spiritual Manifestos: *Visions for Renewed Religious Life in America from Young Spiritual Leaders of Many Faiths*
Edited by *Niles Elliot Goldstein;* Preface by *Martin E. Marty*

Discover the reasons why so many people have kept organized religion at arm's length.

Here, ten young spiritual leaders, most in their mid-thirties, representing the spectrum of religious traditions—Protestant, Catholic, Jewish, Buddhist, Unitarian Universalist—present the innovative ways they are transforming our spiritual communities and our lives. "These ten articulate young spiritual leaders engender hope for the vitality of 21st-century religion." —Forrest Church, Minister of All Souls Church in New York City
6 x 9, 256 pp, HC, ISBN 1-893361-09-8 **$21.95**

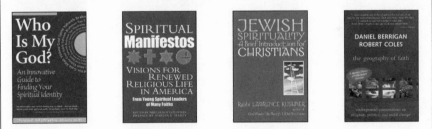

Jewish Spirituality: *A Brief Introduction for Christians*
by *Lawrence Kushner*

Lawrence Kushner, whose award-winning books have brought Jewish spirituality to life for countless readers of all faiths and backgrounds, tailors his unique style to address Christians' questions, revealing the essence of Judaism in a way that people whose own tradition traces its roots to Judaism can understand and enjoy.
5½ x 8½, 112 pp, Quality PB, ISBN 1-58023-150-0 **$12.95**

The Geography of Faith
Underground Conversations on Religious, Political and Social Change
by *Daniel Berrigan* and *Robert Coles;* Updated introduction and afterword by the authors

A classic of faith-based activism—updated for a new generation.

Listen in on the conversations between these two great teachers—one a renegade priest wanted by the FBI for his protests against the Vietnam war, the other a future Pulitzer Prize-winning journalist—as they struggle with what it means to put your faith to the test. Discover how their story of challenging the status quo during a time of great political, religious, and social change is just as applicable to our lives today. 6 x 9, 224 pp, Quality PB, ISBN 1-893361-40-3 **$16.95**

Spiritual Biography

The Life of Evelyn Underhill
An Intimate Portrait of the Groundbreaking Author of Mysticism
by *Margaret Cropper*; Foreword by *Dana Greene*

Evelyn Underhill was a passionate writer and teacher who wrote elegantly on mysticism, worship, and devotional life. This is the story of how she made her way toward spiritual maturity, from her early days of agnosticism to the years when her influence was felt throughout the world. 6 x 9, 288 pp, 5 b/w photos, Quality PB, ISBN 1-893361-70-5 **$18.95**

Zen Effects: *The Life of Alan Watts*
by *Monica Furlong*

The first and only full-length biography of one of the most charismatic spiritual leaders of the twentieth century—now back in print!

Through his widely popular books and lectures, Alan Watts (1915–1973) did more to introduce Eastern philosophy and religion to Western minds than any figure before or since. Here is the only biography of this charismatic figure, who served as Zen teacher, Anglican priest, lecturer, academic, entertainer, a leader of the San Francisco renaissance, and author of more than 30 books, including *The Way of Zen, Psychotherapy East and West* and *The Spirit of Zen*.
6 x 9, 264 pp, Quality PB, ISBN 1-893361-32-2 **$16.95**

Simone Weil: *A Modern Pilgrimage*
by *Robert Coles*

The extraordinary life of the spiritual philosopher who's been called both saint and madwoman.

The French writer and philosopher Simone Weil (1906–1943) devoted her life to a search for God—while avoiding membership in organized religion. Robert Coles' intriguing study of Weil details her short, eventful life, and is an insightful portrait of the beloved and controversial thinker whose life and writings influenced many (from T. S. Eliot to Adrienne Rich to Albert Camus), and continue to inspire seekers everywhere. 6 x 9, 208 pp, Quality PB, ISBN 1-893361-34-9 **$16.95**

Inspired Lives: *Exploring the Role of Faith and Spirituality in the Lives of Extraordinary People*
by *Joanna Laufer* and *Kenneth S. Lewis*

Contributors include *Ang Lee, Wynton Marsalis, Kathleen Norris, Hakeem Olajuwon, Christopher Parkening, Madeleine L'Engle, Doc Watson,* and many more

In this moving book, soul-searching conversations unearth the importance of spirituality and personal faith for more than forty artists and innovators who have made a real difference in our world through their work. 6 x 9, 256 pp, Quality PB, ISBN 1-893361-33-0 **$16.95**

Spiritual Practice

Women Pray
Voices through the Ages, from Many Faiths, Cultures, and Traditions
Edited and with introductions by *Monica Furlong*

Many ways—new and old—to communicate with the Divine.

This beautiful gift book celebrates the rich variety of ways women around the world have called out to the Divine—with words of joy, praise, gratitude, wonder, petition, longing, and even anger—from the ancient world up to our own time. Prayers from women of nearly every religious or spiritual background give us an eloquent expression of what it means to communicate with God. 5 x 7¼,256 pp, Deluxe HC with ribbon marker, ISBN 1-893361-25-X **$19.95**

Praying with Our Hands: *Twenty-One Practices of Embodied Prayer from the World's Spiritual Traditions*
by *Jon M. Sweeney;* Photographs by *Jennifer J. Wilson;*
Foreword by *Mother Tessa Bielecki;* Afterword by *Taitetsu Unno, Ph.D.*

A spiritual guidebook for bringing prayer into our bodies.

This inspiring book of reflections and accompanying photographs shows us twenty-one simple ways of using our hands to speak to God, to enrich our devotion and ritual. All express the various approaches of the world's religious traditions to bringing the body into worship. Spiritual traditions represented include Anglican, Sufi, Zen, Roman Catholic, Yoga, Shaker, Hindu, Jewish, Pentecostal, Eastern Orthodox, and many others.
8 x 8, 96 pp, 22 duotone photographs, Quality PB, ISBN 1-893361-16-0 **$16.95**

The Sacred Art of Listening
Forty Reflections for Cultivating a Spiritual Practice
by *Kay Lindahl;* Illustrations by *Amy Schnapper*

More than ever before, we need to embrace the skills and practice of listening. You will learn to: Speak clearly from your heart • Communicate with courage and compassion • Heighten your awareness for deep listening • Enhance your ability to listen to people with different belief systems. 8 x 8, 160 pp, Illus., Quality PB, ISBN 1-893361-44-6 **$16.95**

Labyrinths from the Outside In
Walking to Spiritual Insight—a Beginner's Guide
by *Donna Schaper* and *Carole Ann Camp*

The user-friendly, interfaith guide to making and using labyrinths— for meditation, prayer, and celebration.

Labyrinth walking is a spiritual exercise *anyone* can do. This accessible guide unlocks the mysteries of the labyrinth for all of us, providing ideas for using the labyrinth walk for prayer, meditation, and celebrations to mark the most important moments in life. Includes instructions for making a labyrinth of your own and finding one in your area.
6 x 9, 208 pp, b/w illus. and photographs, Quality PB, ISBN 1-893361-18-7 **$16.95**

SkyLight Illuminations Series
Andrew Harvey, series editor

Offers today's spiritual seeker an enjoyable entry into the great classic texts of the world's spiritual traditions. Each classic is presented in an accessible translation, with facing pages of guided commentary from experts, giving you the keys you need to understand the history, context, and meaning of the text. This series enables readers of all backgrounds to experience and understand classic spiritual texts directly, and to make them a part of their lives. Andrew Harvey writes the foreword to each volume, an insightful, personal introduction to each classic.

Bhagavad Gita: *Annotated & Explained*
Translation by *Shri Purohit Swami;* Annotation by *Kendra Crossen Burroughs*

"The very best Gita for first-time readers." —Ken Wilber
Millions of people turn daily to India's most beloved holy book, whose universal appeal has made it popular with non-Hindus and Hindus alike. This edition introduces you to the characters; explains references and philosophical terms; shares the interpretations of famous spiritual leaders and scholars; and more. 5½ x 8½, 192 pp, Quality PB, ISBN 1-893361-28-4 **$15.95**

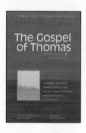

The Way of a Pilgrim: *Annotated & Explained*
Translation and annotation by *Gleb Pokrovsky*

The classic of Russian spirituality—now with facing-page commentary that illuminates and explains the text for you.
This delightful account is the story of one man who sets out to learn the prayer of the heart—also known as the "Jesus prayer"—and how the practice transforms his existence. This edition guides you through an abridged version of the text with facing-page annotations explaining the names, terms and references. 5½ x 8½, 160 pp, Quality PB, ISBN 1-893361-31-4 **$14.95**

The Gospel of Thomas: *Annotated & Explained*
Translation and annotation by *Stevan Davies*

The recently discovered mystical sayings of Jesus—now with facing-page commentary that illuminates and explains the text for you.
Discovered in 1945, this collection of aphoristic sayings sheds new light on the origins of Christianity and the intriguing figure of Jesus, portraying the Kingdom of God as a present fact about the world, rather than a future promise or future threat. This edition guides you through the text with annotations that focus on the meaning of the sayings, ideal for readers with no previous background in Christian history or thought.
5½ x 8½, 192 pp, Quality PB, ISBN 1-893361-45-4 **$15.95**

SkyLight Illuminations Series
Andrew Harvey, series editor

Zohar: *Annotated & Explained*
Translation and annotation by *Daniel C. Matt*

The cornerstone text of Kabbalah, now with facing-page commentary that illuminates and explains the text for you.

The best-selling author of *The Essential Kabbalah* brings together in one place the most important teachings of the *Zohar*, the canonical text of Jewish mystical tradition. Guides readers step by step through the midrash, mystical fantasy and Hebrew scripture that make up the *Zohar*, explaining the inner meanings in facing-page commentary. Ideal for readers without any prior knowledge of Jewish mysticism.
5½ x 8½, 176 pp, Quality PB, ISBN 1-893361-51-9 **$15.95**

Selections from the Gospel of Sri Ramakrishna
Annotated & Explained
Translation by *Swami Nikhilananda*; Annotation by *Kendra Crossen Burroughs*

The words of India's greatest example of God-consciousness and mystical ecstasy in recent history—now with facing-page commentary that illuminates and explains the text for you.

Introduces the fascinating world of the Indian mystic and the universal appeal of his message that has inspired millions of devotees for more than a century. Selections from the original text and insightful yet unobtrusive commentary highlight the most important and inspirational teachings. Ideal for readers without any prior knowledge of Hinduism.
5½ x 8½, 240 pp, b/w photographs, Quality PB, ISBN 1-893361-46-2 **$16.95**

Dhammapada: *Annotated & Explained*
Translation by *Max Müller*; Annotation by *Jack Maguire*

The classic of Buddhist spiritual practice—now with facing-page commentary that illuminates and explains the text for you.

The Dhammapada—words spoken by the Buddha himself over 2,500 years ago—is notoriously difficult to understand for the first-time reader. Now you can experience it with understanding even if you have no previous knowledge of Buddhism. Enlightening facing-page commentary explains all the names, terms, and references, giving you deeper insight into the text. An excellent introduction to Buddhist life and practice.
5½ x 8½, 160 pp, Quality PB, ISBN 1-893361-42-X **$14.95**

Meditation/Prayer

Finding Grace at the Center: *The Beginning of Centering Prayer*
by *M. Basil Pennington, OCSO, Thomas Keating, OCSO,* and *Thomas E. Clarke, SJ*

The book that helped launch the Centering Prayer "movement." Explains the prayer of *The Cloud of Unknowing*, posture and relaxation, the three simple rules of centering prayer, and how to cultivate centering prayer throughout all aspects of your life.
5 x 7¼,112 pp, HC, ISBN 1-893361-69-1 **$14.95**

Three Gates to Meditation Practice
A Personal Journey into Sufism, Buddhism, and Judaism
by *David A. Cooper*

Shows us how practicing within more than one spiritual tradition can lead us to our true home.

Here are over fifteen years from the journey of "post-denominational rabbi" David A. Cooper, author of *God Is a Verb*, and his wife, Shoshana—years in which the Coopers explored a rich variety of practices, from chanting Sufi *dhikr* to Buddhist Vipassanā meditation, to the study of Kabbalah and esoteric Judaism. Their experience demonstrates that the spiritual path is really completely within our reach, whoever we are, whatever we do—as long as we are willing to practice it. 5½ x 8½, 240 pp, Quality PB, ISBN 1-893361-22-5 **$16.95**

Silence, Simplicity & Solitude
A Complete Guide to Spiritual Retreat at Home
by *David A. Cooper*

The classic personal spiritual retreat guide that enables readers to create their own self-guided spiritual retreat at home.

Award-winning author David Cooper traces personal mystical retreat in all of the world's major traditions, describing the varieties of spiritual practices for modern spiritual seekers. Cooper shares the techniques and practices that encompass the personal spiritual retreat experience, allowing readers to enhance their meditation practices and create an effective, self-guided spiritual retreat in their own homes—without the instruction of a meditation teacher. 5½ x 8½, 336 pp, Quality PB, ISBN 1-893361-04-7 **$16.95**

Prayer for People Who Think Too Much
A Guide to Everyday, Anywhere Prayer from the World's Faith Traditions
by *Mitch Finley*

Helps us make prayer a natural part of daily living.

Takes a thoughtful look at how each major faith tradition incorporates prayer into *daily* life. Explores Christian sacraments, Jewish holy days, Muslim daily prayer, "mindfulness" in Buddhism, and more, to help you better understand and enhance your own prayer practices. "I love this book." —Caroline Myss, author of *Anatomy of the Spirit*
5½ x 8½, 224 pp, Quality PB, ISBN 1-893361-21-7 **$16.95**; HC, ISBN 1-893361-00-4 **$21.95**

Children's Spirituality

Where Does God Live?

For ages
3–6

by *August Gold* and *Matthew J. Perlman*

Using simple, everyday examples that children can relate to, this colorful book helps young readers develop a personal understanding of God.

10 x 8½, 32 pp, Quality PB, Full-color photo illus.,
ISBN 1-893361-39-X **$7.95**

God in Between

For ages
4 & up

by *Sandy Eisenberg Sasso*; Full-color illus. by *Sally Sweetland*

If you wanted to find God, where would you look? A magical, mythical tale that teaches that God can be found where we are: within all of us and the relationships between us. "This happy and wondrous book takes our children on a sweet and holy journey into God's presence." —Rabbi Wayne Dosick, Ph.D., author of *The Business Bible* and *Soul Judaism*
9 x 12, 32 pp, HC, Full-color illus., ISBN 1-879045-86-9 **$16.95**

Cain & Abel: *Finding the Fruits of Peace*

For ages
5 & up

by *Sandy Eisenberg Sasso*; Full-color illus. by *Joani Keller Rothenberg*

A sensitive recasting of the ancient tale shows we have the power to deal with anger in positive ways. Provides questions for kids and adults to explore together. "Editor's Choice"—American Library Association's *Booklist* 9 x 12, 32 pp, HC, Full-color illus., ISBN 1-58023-123-3 **$16.95**

In Our Image: *God's First Creatures*

For ages
4 & up

by *Nancy Sohn Swartz*; Full-color illus. by *Melanie Hall*

A playful new twist on the Creation story—from the perspective of the animals. Celebrates the interconnectedness of nature and the harmony of all living things. "The vibrantly colored illustrations nearly leap off the page in this delightful interpretation." —*School Library Journal*
"A message all children should hear, presented in words and pictures that children will find irresistible." —Rabbi Harold Kushner, author of *When Bad Things Happen to Good People*
9 x 12, 32 pp, HC, Full-color illus., ISBN 1-879045-99-0 **$16.95**

Children's Spirituality

Ten Amazing People
And How They Changed the World

For ages 6–10

by *Maura D. Shaw*; Foreword by *Dr. Robert Coles*
Full-color illus. by *Stephen Marchesi*

Black Elk • Dorothy Day • Malcolm X • Mahatma Gandhi • Martin Luther King, Jr. • Mother Teresa • Janusz Korczak • Desmond Tutu • Thich Nhat Hanh • Albert Schweitzer

This vivid, inspirational, and authoritative book will open new possibilities for children by telling the stories of how ten of the past century's greatest leaders changed the world in important ways.

8½, x 11, 48 pp, HC, Full-color illus., ISBN 1-893361-47-0 **$17.95**

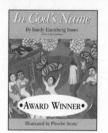

God's Paintbrush

For ages 4 & up

by *Sandy Eisenberg Sasso*; Full-color illus. by *Annette Compton*

Invites children of all faiths and backgrounds to encounter God openly in their own lives. Wonderfully interactive; provides questions adult and child can explore together at the end of each episode. "An excellent way to honor the imaginative breadth and depth of the spiritual life of the young." —Dr. Robert Coles, Harvard University

11 x 8½, 32 pp, HC, Full-color illus., ISBN 1-879045-22-2 **$16.95**

Also available:

A Teacher's Guide 8½ x 11, 32 pp, PB, ISBN 1-879045-57-5 **$8.95**

God's Paintbrush Celebration Kit 9½ x 12, HC, Includes 5 sessions/40 full-color Activity Sheets and Teacher Folder with complete instructions, ISBN 1-58023-050-4 **$21.95**

In God's Name

For ages 4 & up

by *Sandy Eisenberg Sasso*; Full-color illus. by *Phoebe Stone*

Like an ancient myth in its poetic text and vibrant illustrations, this award-winning modern fable about the search for God's name celebrates the diversity and, at the same time, the unity of all the people of the world. "What a lovely, healing book!" —Madeleine L'Engle

9 x 12, 32 pp, HC, Full-color illus., ISBN 1-879045-26-5 **$16.95**

Also available in Spanish:

El nombre de Dios 9 x 12, 32 pp, HC, Full-color illus., ISBN 1-893361-63-2 **$16.95**

Where Does God Live?

For ages 3–6

by *August Gold* and *Matthew J. Perlman*

Using simple, everyday examples that children can relate to, this colorful book helps young readers develop a personal understanding of God.

10 x 8½, 32 pp, Quality PB, Full-color photo illus., ISBN 1-893361-39-X **$7.95**

Religious Etiquette/Reference

How to Be a Perfect Stranger, In 2 Volumes
A Guide to Etiquette in Other People's Religious Ceremonies
Ed. by *Stuart M. Matlins* and *Arthur J. Magida* AWARD WINNERS!

Explains the rituals and celebrations of North America's major religions/denominations, helping an interested guest to feel comfortable, participate to the fullest extent possible, and avoid violating anyone's religious principles. Answers practical questions from the perspective of *any* other faith.

Vol. 1: North America's Largest Faiths

VOL. 1 COVERS: Assemblies of God • Baptist • Buddhist • Christian Church (Disciples of Christ) • Christian Science • Churches of Christ • Episcopalian/Anglican • Greek Orthodox • Hindu • Islam • Jehovah's Witnesses • Jewish • Lutheran • Methodist • Mormon • Presbyterian • Quaker • Roman Catholic • Seventh-day Adventist • United Church of Canada • United Church of Christ 6 x 9, 432 pp, Quality PB, ISBN 1-893361-01-2 **$19.95**

Vol. 2: More Faiths in North America

VOL. 2 COVERS: African American Methodist Churches • Baha'i • Christian and Missionary Alliance • Christian Congregation • Church of the Brethren • Church of the Nazarene • Evangelical Free Church • International Church of the Foursquare Gospel • International Pentecostal Holiness Church • Mennonite/Amish • Native American/First Nations • Orthodox Churches • Pentecostal Church of God • Reformed Church • Sikh • Unitarian Universalist • Wesleyan 6 x 9, 416 pp, Quality PB, ISBN 1-893361-02-0 **$19.95**

Also available:

The Perfect Stranger's Guide to Funerals and Grieving Practices
A Guide to Etiquette in Other People's Religious Ceremonies
Edited by *Stuart M. Matlins*
6 x 9, 240 pp, Quality PB, ISBN 1-893361-20-9 **$16.95**

The Perfect Stranger's Guide to Wedding Ceremonies
A Guide to Etiquette in Other People's Religious Ceremonies
Edited by *Stuart M. Matlins*
6 x 9, 208 pp, Quality PB, ISBN 1-893361-19-5 **$16.95**

Other Interesting Books—Spirituality

God Within: *Our Spiritual Future — As Told by Today's New Adults*
Edited by *Jon M. Sweeney* and *the Editors at SkyLight Paths*

Our faith, in our words.

The future of spirituality in America lies in the vision of the women and men who are the children of the "baby boomer" generation—born into the post–New-Age world of the 1970s and 1980s. This book gives voice to their spiritual energy, and allows readers of all ages to share in their passionate quests for faith and belief. This thought-provoking collection of writings, poetry, and art showcases the voices that are defining the future of religion, faith, and belief as we know it. 6 x 9, 176 pp, Quality PB, ISBN 1-893361-15-2 **$14.95**

Releasing the Creative Spirit: *Unleash the Creativity in Your Life*
by *Dan Wakefield*

From the author of *How Do We Know When It's God?*—
a practical guide to accessing creative power in every area of your life.

Explodes the myths associated with the creative process and shows how everyone can uncover and develop their natural ability to create. Drawing on religion, psychology, and the arts, Dan Wakefield teaches us that the key to creation of any kind is clarity—of body, mind, and spirit—and he provides practical exercises that each of us can do to access that centered quality that allows creativity to shine. 7 x 10, 256 pp, Quality PB, ISBN 1-893361-36-5 **$16.95**

Spiritual Innovators: *Seventy-Five Extraordinary People Who Changed the World in the Past Century*
Edited by *Ira Rifkin* and *the Editors at SkyLight Paths*; Foreword by *Robert Coles*

Black Elk, H. H. the Dalai Lama, Abraham Joshua Heschel, Krishnamurti, C. S. Lewis, Thomas Merton, Elijah Muhammad, Aimee Semple McPherson, Martin Luther King, Jr., Simone Weil, and many more.

Profiles of the most important spiritual leaders of the past one hundred years. An invaluable reference of twentieth-century religion and an inspiring resource for spiritual challenge today. Authoritative list of seventy-five includes mystics and martyrs, intellectuals and charismatics from the East and West. For each, includes a brief biography, inspiring quotes and resources for more in-depth study.
6 x 9, 304 pp, b/w photographs, Quality PB, ISBN 1-893361-50-0 **$16.95**;
HC, ISBN 1-893361-43-8 **$24.95**

Or phone, fax, mail or e-mail to: SKYLIGHT PATHS Publishing
Sunset Farm Offices, Route 4 • P.O. Box 237 • Woodstock, Vermont 05091
Tel: (802) 457-4000 • Fax: (802) 457-4004 • www.skylightpaths.com
Credit card orders: (800) 962-4544 (8:30AM–5:30PM ET Monday–Friday)
Generous discounts on quantity orders. SATISFACTION GUARANTEED. Prices subject to change.